REMY'S KITCHEN

Celebration

Easy Step by Step
Recipes from a Masterchef
Junior Finalist

Remy Powell

Text by Remy Powell

with Tracey Broussard

Foreword by Linda Ellerbee

Photographs courtesy Tracey Broussard, the Powell Collection, MasterChef Junior, and The Florida Future Chef Student Cookoff

Published by First Flight Books

35 34 33 32 31 30 29 28 27 26 1 2 3 4 5

ISBN: 978-1-887229-68-5

Published by First Flight Books

firstflightbooks.net

Table of Contents

FOREWORD

SCARY PLACES

As a kid, I was taught the kitchen was a scary place. Bad stuff happened in there. People got burned, cut. Dropped things. Broke objects. Like glasses. Plates. Food. Food got broken a lot. Plus, there were numbers. Cooking wanted me to use math. I hated math. Numbers confused me the way words never did.

I decided to stay out of the kitchen. My mother agreed.

And so, if it were not for books, I would never ever have learned to cook—and then learned to love to cook.

If I'd known how much I would come to love cooking, how much time I would think about food, taste food, dream about food—play WITH my food—I would have known how much I needed a Chef Remy in my life.

Kids weren't supposed to go near the making of food. Too dangerous. A kitchen is no place for a kid. Can't trust kids with knives and meat pounders and scissors and stoves...no, siree. NO stoves.

But I believed then as I believe now that ignorance is not bliss.

And kids aren't dumb.

For 25 years, we produced a television documentary series for kids based on the assumption that kids were smart, and if you showed them respect by teaching them new things, they showed respect by learning new things.

Once, we had a famous chef on our show. He was supposed to show kids how to make healthy after school snacks (using no fire nor knives, mind you). Healthy and tasty. Uh-huh. The very famous chef showed kids how to make a Caesar Salad. I said I knew what made it healthy, but what made it tasty? I mean, a Caesar Salad is not going to replace Kool-Aid. And Twinkies. The famous chef said to add a cup of sugar to the salad dressing.

Well, yeah, but...

Remy was the teacher those kids needed. She was the teacher I needed, the one who would say to me...

> *Come on in this kitchen, girl. This is where the real fun is. Look what I can do with a ball of dough. Here. Make some bread. You can do it. This is a stove. You'll bake in that. Wait until you smell your bread baking. By the way, that stove can burn down the house, so you need to learn how to use it safely. And you can do that. You're not stupid, just young.*

See this knife. This is the coolest thing, a special knife. A chef's knife. You're going to be careful with this knife because the knife opens the most secret doors to the magic of cooking.

This spoon? It's for tasting the magic with your brain, the magic you make with your hands. Figuring it out.

Fire, a knife, and a brain. That's what you need.

Actually, that's all you need.

Except, of course, for someone like Chef Remy. You need Chef Remy. You don't get called Chef by accident, or because you have blue eyes or a sweet smile. You get called Chef if you are one. Remy Willow Powell is. She paid her dues, learned cooking from her grandmother, her mother and other family members. Remy has television experience, radio, podcast, and book experience.

And teaching experience.

By that, I mean she has experience teaching YOU! The past teaches the young, see. And then the young teach the old.

Lovely how that works. Chef Remy, take it from here...

— Linda Ellerbee

Writer, television producer, and journalist

REMY

INTRODUCTION

If I can cook, you can cook!

I've been helping my Bubbe (that's my grandma) in the kitchen since I was two. But here's a secret: I didn't want to touch the oven or stove until I was nine! I was really nervous at first. But two days later, I took a deep breath and made scrambled eggs. That was a big deal. After that, cooking started to feel way easier. Once you do one thing, it's like, boom, you start getting better and better.

Eggs are special to my family because my great-grandma Coco started with eggs too. She found a recipe for egg salad and made it for her brothers and sisters. They couldn't believe how good it was! And just like that, eggs made my family know her as an amazing cook.

I wasn't nervous by then—and cooking was nothing but fun. That's when someone from *MasterChef Junior* saw a picture of me on my Bubbe's Instagram. I was helping make a pie, and they thought I might be a good contestant. And just like that, everything changed.

I promise that there's no better feeling in the world as good as feeding delicious food to the people you love. I'm here to help you do that.

My recipes will bring good vibes to the kitchen—and they definitely bring people to the table! I've added fun twists and easy little hacks to help you have fun while you cook. My family is totally obsessed with these dishes, and I really hope you love them too.

The recipes are grouped by holidays and special times of year, starting the party with Mardi Gras and going all the way to New Year's Eve. I love cooking for each season because it's not just about food—it's about making memories. And don't worry, I didn't forget the drinks! Every menu comes with a special drink to make things feel extra festive.

I'm so excited to share these recipes with you. If you make any of them, I'd *love* to see! Snap a pic of your dish (or you with your dish!) and tag me on Instagram @Chefremypowell.

Happy cooking and have fun!

—Chef Remy

Lagniappe

Lagniappe (say it like this: *lan-yap*) is a word you hear a lot in Louisiana. It means a little something extra. When you see the word Lagniappe after my recipes, it's your sign that extra information is coming your way!

REMY'S RULES FOR COOKING

1. **Expect the unexpected.** Mistakes happen and things don't always turn out the way you want them to.

2. **Always have a backup plan.** Sometimes things don't go the way you planned. Don't panic! Think about how you can fix it or turn it into something else. Can you turn it into a snack? Add a new topping? Call it "rustic" and roll with it? The goal is to learn, not to be perfect—and to never waste good food (or a good mood).

3. **Keep it simple.** You don't have to make a million things. Just one thing made well is all you need.

4. **Don't cross-contaminate.** Pay attention to food safety rules. Many foods (I'm talking to you, chicken.) carry bacteria. Make sure you follow recommended safety rules such as using different cutting boards for meats and vegetables or fruits.

5. **Mix it up!** When you're cooking, think about how everything tastes *and* feels. Does it need something crunchy? Something creamy? A little sweet with the salty? Balancing flavors and textures make your dish way more fun to eat—and way more delicious.

6. **Keep it local.** Keep it local. Your food will taste much better if you buy local and seasonal ingredients. It usually costs less money and is better for the Earth, too.

7. **Think out of the box.** Use whatever you have in the pantry. Make a game of creating new dishes. Try not to waste anything.

8. **Mis en place means everything in its place.** Line up your ingredients, measure them and have everything at your fingertips before you start cooking. It makes your experience so much more fun if you take the time to get things ready.

9. **We eat with our eyes first!** Making your food look awesome is just as fun as making it taste good. You don't need fancy stuff—check out your local dollar store, craft store, or even a thrift shop for cute plates and platters. After the holidays, you can find fun stuff on sale (*super* cheap!). That's a great time to grab things for later. Red sprinkles for Christmas? Boom—they also work for Valentine's Day too!

10. **Cook from your heart.** Love is my secret ingredient. When you cook with love, mistakes don't matter.

CHARBOODIE BOARD

My little sister, Rory, called Charcuterie boards "Char-boo-dee" boards for at least a year until she learned how to say it right. Our whole family calls them Charboodie boards now.

Whatever you call them, they're one of the best things you can make for a party or family gathering. They're fun to create, look pretty and have something for everyone. They're like an edible art project that even your baby sister can help you put together.

Begin with a nice board or platter to arrange your goodies on.

Next, make sure you have foods that are lots of different colors, shapes and sizes. Keep it fun!

REMY'S SPECIAL SEASONINGS MIX

You won't need to prepare this mix to make any of my recipes, but you'll find it useful for some. And having some on hand might inspire you to make your own recipes.

Ingredients

- 2 tablespoons salt
- 2 teaspoons finely ground black pepper
- ½ teaspoon cayenne pepper
- ½ tablespoon granulated garlic
- ½ tablespoons granulated onion
- ½ teaspoon dried, ground thyme
- ½ teaspoon dried, ground oregano
- ½ teaspoon dried, ground basil
- ½ teaspoon Spanish paprika

Instructions

1. Makes about ⅓ cup

2. Combine all ingredients in a sealable container, close and shake to blend. Be creative and change any of the herbs to the ones you prefer, keeping the same amounts.

3. This is one of my favorite gifts for friends and family. I use small pretty jars and tie them with colorful ribbons. You can find personal labels on the internet.

MARDI GRAS

Mardi Gras in New Orleans is *SO* much fun—and I'm super lucky that my family gets to go almost every year! We always stay at my great-grandma Coco's house, which is right near the parade routes. People on the floats throw out beads, toys, stuffed animals, even light-up things—and yes, we try to catch *all* of it! Between parades, we bring our loot inside and show it off to Coco. Then she feeds us her famous red beans and rice—New Orleans classic (and one of my favorites).

My Bubbe grew up in St. Bernard Parish, so we also have to catch a parade there, too. My Great Aunt Stacey and Uncle Alfie always take us to a restaurant called Brewster's, which our cousin Ted owns. We park there, grab big, juicy burgers, and get ready for the floats to roll by. The grown-ups love Brewster's special drink called a Boomalache. If you ever visit and try one, let me know if it's good—I'm sticking with lemonade.

New Orleans is super famous for its Cajun and Creole food, and Mardi Gras is the *perfect* reason to get in the kitchen and try something new. So, grab your apron, put on some music, and let's get cookin'!

Bon appétit! Or like we say down here: *Laissez les bon temps rouler!*

(That's fancy French for "Let the good times roll!")

- Shrimp and Grits with Tasso Cream
- Sweet Calas
- Easy King Cakes
- Boom Chicka Boom

SHRIMP AND GRITS WITH TASSO CREAM

Serves 6

This is my family's favorite brunch recipe, but it's great at any meal. Rich and creamy grits are topped with one of the most incredibly flavorful shrimp and cream sauces you will ever taste.

It calls for Tasso ham, which is a smoked, spiced and cured meat popular in Louisiana. If you can't find it, you can substitute regular ham.

Shrimp & Cream Sauce, Remy Style

Okay, so this recipe is a twist from one of the best New Orleans cookbooks called *New Orleans Classic Celebrations* by Kit Wohl. The original was created by a super-talented chef named Donald Link—he's one of my Bubbe's absolute favorites! He's won big awards from the James Beard Foundation (it's like the Oscars of food).

One of my dreams? To win a James Beard Award, too. Maybe they'll make a special category for kid cookbooks—how cool would that be?! If you like this book, maybe write to them and tell them I should be nominated. (Just sayin'.)

Now let's talk shrimp. I HATE—like capital H hate—de-veining shrimp. Some folks in New Orleans don't bother with it, but honestly... ew. If you want to skip the ick, buy shrimp that are already de-veined. Fresh shrimp are awesome, but frozen ones work great too and are usually easier to find (and cheaper). If you *do* need to de-vein them, just smile sweetly and ask a parent or older sibling to help. (Tell them it's a bonding moment.)

If you can find wild Gulf shrimp—grab them! They're super tasty and have the best texture. But if not, try to get wild-caught shrimp from somewhere nearby. It'll make your dish taste way better, promise.

HERE'S A TIP: The best way to make this recipe is to cook your stock first and let it cool while you do everything else. Don't want to make stock? No worries—use chicken broth instead! It won't be *as* rich, but it'll still be delicious. I know, because I'd totally eat it either way.

Shrimp Stock

- 20 large unpeeled Gulf shrimp
- 1 small onion
- 4 cloves garlic
- 4 cups water
- Salt and pepper

Peel and de-vein shrimp. Set aside. Combine shells and remaining ingredients in a small stockpot or saucepan and bring to a boil. Lower to a simmer and cook for an additional 10 to 15 minutes. Strain the stock into a bowl using a fine mesh strainer.

Lagniappe

If you've got extra shrimp stock—don't throw it out! Pour it into a container (or even an ice cube tray!) and freeze it for later. You can use it to make rice taste like it came from a fancy restaurant, or to add extra yumminess to soups and sauces when you're cooking anything with seafood.

It's like saving a little magic for your next meal.

Shrimp and Tasso Cream

- 3 tablespoons butter
- 1/4 cup diced onion
- 1/4 cup diced celery
- 1/4 cup diced Tasso ham
- 1 1/2 teaspoon chopped fresh thyme
- 1/4 plus 1/8 teaspoon cayenne pepper
- 1/4 plus 1/8 teaspoon paprika
- 1 teaspoon chopped garlic
- 2 tablespoons flour
- 1/2 cup shrimp stock (or more if needed to thin)
- 1/2 cup heavy cream
- Dash lemon juice
- Dash hot sauce
- 3 tablespoons canola oil
- 20 large Gulf shrimp, peeled and deveined as instructed above
- 3/4 teaspoon salt
- 3/4 teaspoon ground pepper
- Chopped chives for garnish

1. Start by melting 2 tablespoons of butter in a medium saucepan over medium heat. Once it's melted, toss in your onion, celery, ham, thyme, cayenne, and paprika. Stir it all around and let it cook for a few minutes, just until the veggies start to soften and smell *amazing*.

2. Next, add the garlic and keep stirring for another couple of minutes. (Don't let the garlic burn—it cooks fast!)

3. Then, add the last tablespoon of butter and let it melt right into everything. Now here comes the fun part: we're making a roux! (Say it like this: "roo." Like kangaroo without the kang.)

What's a Roux?

A roux is a super important part of lots of creamy sauces. It's made by mixing butter and flour together to thicken everything up. It turns your dish from watery to wow.

1. So once that last bit of butter is melted, sprinkle in your flour and stir, stir, stir! Keep mixing it around with a spoon or spatula until everything is combined and smooth—no lumps! It'll start out pale and then get a little golden. That's when you know you're on your way to something seriously tasty.

2. Gradually add the shrimp stock and reduce it by half. Add the cream and reduce, stirring occasionally until the sauce has thickened. Remove from heat and stir in the lemon juice and hot sauce.

3. Heat the canola oil over medium heat in a large saucepan until it's hot but not smoking. Salt and pepper the shrimp, then add to the pan. Cook for about two minutes on each side and drain excess oil from the pan. Pour the gravy over the shrimp, reduce heat to low and simmer for another 5 minutes. Taste and adjust salt and pepper.

Lagniappe

This shrimp and Tasso cream is so good, it can go with just about anything. Try it tossed with pasta or spooned over a fluffy pile of rice. No matter how you plate it, it's creamy, savory, and full of big New Orleans flavor. Trust me, your taste buds are going be doing a happy dance.

Creamy Grits

There are so many fun and creative ways to make grits, but this version is one of my favorites. It's warm, buttery, and extra creamy—like a hug in a bowl. The idea for this recipe was inspired by the *amazing* grits at Zea's in New Orleans (if you've been, you know!).

Whether you serve them with shrimp, eggs, or just eat them by the spoonful, these grits are total comfort food.

Ingredients:

- 1 cup heavy cream
- 1 cup chicken stock
- 2 tablespoons butter
- ½ cup 5-minute grits, preferably Jim Dandy brand
- Salt to taste

Bring the cream to a boil. Add the chicken stock and bring to a boil again. Add the butter and a little salt. Add the grits. Turn the heat to low and simmer for five minutes. Taste and adjust salt.

To plate: Make three small circles of grits. Make craters using the back of a spoon. Fill the craters with Tasso gravy and then place the shrimp. Garnish with chives.

Lagniappe

Grits can be like a blank canvas before you paint on it. Your "colors" are the tasty bites you either place on top or stir into them. Many people love to add cheddar cheese or a cheese blend. Consider stirring in some finely chopped jalapeno or serrano chiles and some Parmesan cheese. Serve "loaded" grits in places where you would normally have rice or a potato—with roast chicken, a perfectly cooked medium rare steak, and of course as a side for eggs and bacon, eggs and corned beef hash, fried green tomatoes. Grits go everywhere! Just like big hugs.

SWEET CALAS

Serves 4

Calas (say it like: *kah-lahs*) are awesome little Creole rice fritters made with leftover rice, sugar, and eggs—then sprinkled with powdered sugar like donut snow!

They've been around forever in New Orleans, but for a while, people kind of forgot about them... until Ms. Poppy Tooker, a super cool culinary activist, brought them back! Thanks, Ms. Poppy!

Eating calas is like taking a bite out of history (a really yummy bite). You can make them sweet or savory depending on your mood—or what you're having them with. I like mine sweet, of course!

This is actually *Ms. Tooker's* recipe, and it was one of the very first things I made when I was auditioning for *MasterChef Junior*. Pretty cool, right?

Ingredients:

- 2 cups cooked rice
- 6 tablespoons flour
- 3 heaping tablespoons sugar
- 2 teaspoons baking powder
- ¼ teaspoon salt
- 2 eggs
- ¼ teaspoon vanilla
- Vegetable oil (for deep frying)
- Confectioner's (powdered) sugar

1. In a bowl, combine rice, flour, sugar, baking powder and salt. Mix until the rice is coated with dry ingredients. Add eggs and vanilla and mix well.

2. Add about an inch of vegetable oil to a frying pan and heat on medium to 360 degrees. Carefully drop rice mixture by the spoonful into the hot oil.

3. Fry for about two minutes or until golden brown. Remove from the oil with a slotted spoon and drain on paper towels.

4. Sprinkle with confectioner's sugar. Serve hot.

***NOTE:** Hot oil is dangerous, and you should never, ever attempt to fry something without an adult's help.

EASY KING CAKES

Serves 8

In New Orleans we eat these sweet, colorful cakes all through Mardi Gras! A King Cake is kind of like a giant cinnamon roll—*but better*—and there's a tiny plastic baby hidden inside. If you find the baby in your slice, guess what? You get to bring the next King Cake! (And yes, that's *totally* a win.)

Traditional King Cakes are made with fancy yeasted dough, but I've got a shortcut that's just as yummy and way easier. Ready for the hack? Pillsbury Flaky Cinnamon Rolls. Boom. You just shape them into a circle, bake them, and then go wild with icing and sprinkles.

The sprinkles are the *most fun part*—we make our own in purple, green, and gold, the official colors of Mardi Gras. They make the cake sparkle, and the whole thing looks like a party on a plate. Trust me, you *need* to try this. It's fun, sweet, and totally magical.

Ingredients:

- 2 cans Pillsbury Flaky Cinnamon Rolls with Buttercream Frosting (Store brands sometimes don't puff up the same way Pillsbury does, therefore I highly recommend that you use this brand.)
- 1 cup granulated sugar
- Purple, green and yellow food color

1. Preheat oven to 375 degrees.

2. Line a baking sheet with parchment paper or a silicone baking sheet.

3. Open the cinnamon roll package and separate the rolls. Smoosh them down a little so they look more like ovals than circles.

4. Place them on the baking sheet so they form a big oval. Leave a little room between each roll, because they expand as they bake.

5. Bake in the preheated oven for about 12 minutes. You want them to be golden brown. They should not be gooey.

Decorating Your Easy King Cake!

1. While your cinnamon rolls are baking, let's get those sprinkles ready!

2. Grab three small bowls and scoop equal amounts of sugar into each one (about 2–3 tablespoons per bowl works great).

3. Add purple food coloring to one bowl, green to the second, and yellow (or gold) to the third.

4. If you're using gel or paste food coloring, just one or two tiny drops should do the trick.

5. If you're using the liquid kind from the grocery store, you might need a few more drops to get those bold Mardi Gras colors. Just stir and see what you like, bright or pastel, it's all good!

6. When your cinnamon roll "cake" is done baking, take it out and let it cool for about 5 minutes (just enough so the frosting doesn't melt into a puddle).

7. Now grab that buttercream frosting from the cinnamon roll can and spread it over the top while it's still warm and gooey—but not hot! Then sprinkle your colorful sugar on top in sections or stripes for that classic King Cake look.

8. And don't forget to hide the tiny baby inside (before you frost it if you're feeling sneaky)!

9. Now for the fun part. Sprinkle a strip of purple sugar on top of the cake. Now make a strip of green sugar. Next, you guessed it, is the yellow sugar. Keep doing this going around the cake until the entire top looks gorgeous with Mardi Gras colors.

Let's Talk Babies & Minis!

You can order a little bag of plastic babies online (they're tiny and cute). BUT! Make sure you tell everyone eating the cake that there's something hidden inside. Nobody wants a surprise crunch from a plastic baby.

No baby? No problem! You can also use a big, dried lima bean instead. After your cake is baked and cooled a bit, gently push the baby or bean into the bottom of the cake. Leave a little clue showing where it went in, so whoever finds it knows they've won!

Bonus Idea: Want to make mini-King Cakes? Bake the cinnamon rolls separately like usual, then use a small cookie cutter to cut a little circle in the middle to make them look like tiny wreaths. Frost them and sprinkle with your Mardi Gras sugars just like the big one. Everyone gets their own cute, colorful cake!

BOOM CHICKA BOOM

Serves 1

Our cousin, Jessica, gave me Brewster's recipe for a special kid's drink called Boom Chicka Boom. It calls for making your own ginger syrup and raspberry syrup. Don't let this scare you. Making syrups to flavor your drinks is easy and fun.

Ingredients:

- ¾ ounce raspberry syrup *
- ¾ ounce ginger syrup *
- 4 ounces sour mix (Available in the soda or mixer aisle of your supermarket.)
- 4 ounces club soda
- Raspberries to garnish, if desired

1. Fill a chilled glass with ice. Add the raspberry syrup and the ginger syrup. Add sour mix and stir. Top with club soda and gently stir. Garnish with fresh raspberries.

Ginger Syrup

Makes 2 Cups

- 1 medium knob ginger, peeled and thinly sliced
- 2 cups water
- 2 cups sugar

1. Combine all ingredients in a small saucepan and simmer until the ginger is translucent. Strain and cool. Store in a covered container in the refrigerator.

Raspberry Syrup

Makes 3 cups

- 1 ½ cups fresh raspberries, rinsed
- 2 cups water
- 1 cup granulated sugar

1. Bring all ingredients to a boil in a small saucepan. Reduce heat and let simmer until the raspberries begin to fall apart and lose their color. Let cool.
2. Strain into a covered container. Store in the refrigerator.

VALENTINE'S DAY

Bring on the heart-shaped candy boxes, squishy stuffed animals, glittery cards, and pretty flowers! Valentine's Day isn't just for couples anymore—it's a day to celebrate *all kinds* of love: your family, your friends, your pets (yes, even your dog who steals snacks), and most of all... *yourself!*

And what better way to show some love than by making sweet, homemade treats straight from the heart? Whether you're baking for someone special or just because it's Tuesday and you love sprinkles, these Valentine's Day goodies are guaranteed to make smiles.

Bonus points if you stick to the Valentine color theme! Think red, white, and pink everything—from berries and frosting to drinks and dips.

Here are a few of my family's favorite Valentine's recipes to get you started.

Get ready to feel the love (and maybe a little sugar rush)!

* Valentine's Candy Charboodie Board
* Shrimp Cocktails
* One-Bowl Brownies
* Strawberry Lemonade

VALENTINE'S CANDY CHARBOODIE BOARD

Valentine's Day might *just* be the best holiday for making a candy "char-BOO-die" board. Why? Because the candy is SO fun—all those hearts, pinks, reds, and sparkles!

1. Grab a mix of your faves: sweet, sour, chewy, chocolatey, marshmallowy—the more variety, the better. And don't skip the Conversation Hearts! They're not just cute, they have silly sayings on them that are *so* fun to read. Some even have texting phrases like "LOL" and "TTYL." (Not that I'd know... I don't even have a phone yet. Thanks, Mom and Dad.)

2. Want to take your board to the next level? Add some chocolate-covered strawberries, cookies, or even mini cupcakes! There are *no rules* here, just have fun and share the love.

SHRIMP COCKTAILS

Serves 4

Valentine's Day is all about love—and what's not to love about shrimp cocktail? It's got all the Valentine's colors: pink and white shrimp with red cocktail sauce—totally on theme and *totally tasty*. I *love* cocktail sauce, and making your own is way easier than you'd think.

REMY'S HACK: Grab a ready-made tray of boiled, peeled shrimp from the grocery store or big box store—super simple. Then wow everyone by saying, "Oh yeah, I made the cocktail sauce myself." Instant legend status.

Now here's the fun part. This recipe is super special to me because it's something I make with my Nana Sue and Uncle Dave whenever we visit them in Fort Pierce, Florida. I have the *best* time there playing on the beach, raiding Nana's closet (hello vintage sunglasses!), and learning how to cook with her. She's amazing at making even a regular dinner feel like a celebration.

Uncle Dave's job? He's the master of restaurant ordering. He always knows *exactly* what to get. But when we're home, this shrimp cocktail with Nana's jumbo shrimp and our homemade sauce is always a hit—and *so* much fun to serve.

So now it's your turn to make a memory.
Shrimp + sauce + love = the perfect Valentine's story to share at your table.

Cocktail Sauce

- 1 cup ketchup
- 2 to 3 tablespoons prepared horseradish
- 1 tablespoon lemon juice
- Salt to taste
- Optional: Hot sauce
- Lemon wedges for garnish

1. Mix all ingredients into the ketchup in a small bowl. Begin by adding two tablespoons of prepared horseradish. Taste and adjust for more horseradish or salt. Add a few shakes of hot sauce if you like it spicy.

2. Arrange the shrimp on a pretty plate or platter with a bowl of cocktail sauce in the middle. If you want to get extra fancy, shred some lettuce and put it at the bottom of a Champagne coupe—that's the Champagne glass that is wide and shallow. Top the lettuce with cocktail sauce and arrange the shrimp around the rim of the glass. Garnish the plate or the Champagne glasses with a lemon wedge. So pretty!

ONE-BOWL BROWNIES

Let me tell you a sweet story...

We have a family friend named Dr. Melissa—and she's seriously amazing. Like, went-to-med-school, takes-care-of-heroes-at-the-V.A., superhero-in-real-life kind of amazing. But here's the twist... Dr. Melissa can't cook. Not At All.

So, my Bubbe created this brownie recipe *just* for her—super easy, super chocolatey, and you only need one bowl to make it. That's right. No fancy equipment. No big cleanup. And guess what? Dr. Melissa totally nailed it. If she can do it, you definitely can too.

And here's my favorite part:

Dr. Melissa makes these brownies to share with the awesome nurses she works with. And you can do the same! Bake up a batch and surprise your teacher, bus driver, or the crossing guard.

Everyone deserves a little homemade sunshine. And nothing says *you matter* like something sweet made with love (and lots of chocolate chips).

Go ahead—bake, share, repeat. You'll be the brownie hero of the day.

Ingredients:

- 1 cup granulated sugar
- ½ cup all-purpose flour
- ⅓ cup cocoa powder
- ¼ teaspoon baking powder
- ¼ teaspoon salt
- 2 eggs
- ½ cup vegetable oil
- 1 teaspoon vanilla
- Cooking spray
- Get out your measuring cups, measuring spoons, one big bowl, a cup or little bowl and an 8 × 8" pan. Also get out the wire rack for cooling

1. Preheat the oven to 350 degrees.
2. Spray an 8 x 8" square pan with cooking spray.
3. Combine one cup of sugar, ½ cup of flour, ⅓ cup of cocoa powder, ¼ teaspoon baking powder and ¼ teaspoon salt in a big bowl. Whisk them together. When a recipe says whisk, it just means to mix together really well. You can use a fork if you don't have a whisk (just don't tell Chef Gordon I said so).
4. Crack an egg into a small bowl or cup. You do this in case you get shells. It's way easier than digging shells out of the big bowl. Don't ask me how I know this.
5. Pour the egg into the big bowl.
6. Crack the next egg in the little cup, then pour into the big bowl.
7. Add ½ cup of oil and 1 teaspoon vanilla to the big bowl.
8. Mix it all together until everything is all dark, smooth and chocolatey.

9. Pour it into the pan.

10. Use the spatula to scrape all the batter from the bowl into the pan. Spatulas are my favorite kitchen tool. I have a collection of them. One day I will have a spatula line with my face on them...

11. Put the pan into the heated oven. Bake for 20-25 minutes for a good gooey brownie. If you like a firm, cakier brownie, bake a little longer. This might take some trial and error.

12. Remove from the oven and let sit for 5 minutes.

13. Put the wire rack on top of the pan, Using potholders, hold the bottom of the pan and the rack. Carefully flip it over so that the brownies are now on the rack instead of in the pan.

14. Let cool for about 20 minutes.

Let's Slice and Remix!

Once your brownies are baked and cooled (the hard part is waiting, I know!), it's time to slice them into squares.

PRO TIP: Use a sharp knife and run it under hot water between cuts. That way, your slices stay neat, and the brownies don't stick to the knife. (Sticky knives = messy squares = sad faces. We can't have that.)

Now that you've mastered the classic version, it's time to get creative! Want to make them even more chocolatey? Stir in a handful of chocolate chips, chopped candy bars, or even marshmallows. Go wild—this is your brownie adventure.

Halloween Hack: Line the bottom of the pan with Oreos before you pour in the batter. It makes a super cool crunchy surprise layer that everyone loves. Spoooooky good.

Make it Pretty: Before baking, sprinkle some festive sprinkles on top for extra sparkle and fun. Because why not?

HEADS UP: If you're adding stuff, you may need to bake a little longer. To check if they're done, stick a toothpick in the center. If it comes out clean (no gooey batter), they're ready!

Now cut, share, and get ready for everyone to ask, "Wait, *you* made these?!"

STRAWBERRY LEMONADE

Serves 1

We're staying on theme with a pink drink here. What's even better than pink lemonade? Lemonade that's made with lemon sparkling water. If you want to be extra, top it with cotton candy. You're welcome.

Ingredients:

- ½ large lemon, squeezed
- 1 tablespoon plus 1 ½ teaspoons granulated sugar
- 2 strawberries
- ¾ cup cold lemon-flavored sparkling water
- Suggested garnishes: Pink cotton candy, lemon wheel, straw and/or umbrella.

Combine lemon juice, sugar and strawberries in a cocktail shaker or big plastic cup. Muddle (that means smash it really good) the berries and mix everything together. Fill a glass with ice and pour the strawberry and lemon mixture onto the ice. Top it with sparkling water. Stir carefully. Top with cotton candy. Garnish with a lemon wheel, pretty straw and paper umbrella.

Lagniappe

Lemon wheel: To make a lemon wheel, cut round slices from the lemon and then make a cut from the center of the wheel outwards. This is the part you will use to make the lemon stay on the glass.

ST. PATRICK'S DAY

My sister, Rory, was born **two days** before St. Patrick's Day. This gives us an excuse to celebrate her even longer, since St. Patrick's Day is all about having fun with your family and friends. We also have some Irish in our family tree, which gives us even more reason to party.

You don't have to be Irish to celebrate St. Patrick's Day, or to have the luck of the Irish. Make my recipes and good luck will come to you.

Just watch out for those pesky leprechauns (and little sisters).

They will steal your shortbread and pinch you if you're not wearing green.

* Slowcooker Corned Beef
* Irish Style Boiled Cabbage and Potatoes
* Meyer Lemon Shortbread
* Shamrock Shake

SLOW COOKER CORNED BEEF

Serves 6

This dish is an *Irish classic*—and totally perfect for St. Patrick's Day! Corned beef is already packed with flavor, so it doesn't need a ton of extra seasoning. You just pop it in the slow cooker and let the magic happen.

Even though the recipe uses a little beer, don't worry, it's totally safe for kids! Once it's cooked, all the alcohol goes *poof!* and disappears, leaving behind just the flavor. (Kind of like a cooking trick!)

And here's the best part: the leftovers are even *better*. Slice it up and make corned beef sandwiches on rye bread the next day. Add some mustard or pickles if you're feeling fancy. Trust me, you'll be counting down to lunchtime.

So, grab your green apron and let's get cooking—your taste buds are going to do a happy dance!

Ingredients:

- 1 3-pound corned beef
- 1 onion peeled and cut in half
- 1 12-ounce beer of choice
- Water (My dad uses beef broth instead of water here. Try both ways and see what you like best.)

1. Unwrap the corned beef from the package. It'll have a package of pickling spices with it. Set the pickling spices aside for now. Place the beef in the bottom of a slow cooker.

2. Sprinkle the pickling spices all over the beef, add the onion then pour the beer into the slow cooker.

3. Add enough water so the beef is completely covered.

4. Put the lid on the cooker and set the temperature to low.

5. Cook for at least 8 hours, or until the meat is fork tender (That means when you stick a fork in it, the meat immediately starts to come apart.)

IRISH-STYLE BOILED CABBAGE & POTATOES

Serves 6

Nothing goes better with corned beef than good ol' cabbage and potatoes. This recipe comes straight from my great-great Grandma Laura, and it's been passed down through the family like a pot of gold!

My Bubbe started making it every St. Patrick's Day when she married my Paw-Paw Marty. But guess who loved it the most? Paw-Paw Marty's mom, Safta—who just happened to be Jewish! Every year, she'd call Bubbe around St. Patrick's Day and say, *"When are you making the cabbage and potatoes?"* She never missed that dinner.

Some people throw the cabbage and potatoes right into the slow cooker with the corned beef. I'm just going say it... please don't! It might save time, but the flavor just isn't the same. Cooking them separately makes everything taste way better—promise.

Here's the trick: Salt the cabbage and potatoes *while* they cook, then give them a little more love (a.k.a. salt and butter) when they're done. And if you've got some Irish butter, definitely use it—it's next-level yum. You can even use vegan butter if that's your thing.

Simple, classic, and so delicious you'll want seconds. Maybe even thirds.

Ingredients:

- 8 Yukon gold or russet potatoes, washed and peeled
- 1 head of cabbage, washed and outer leaves torn off
- Water to cover cabbage and potatoes
- ½ stick butter
- 2 teaspoons salt plus more salt to taste

1. Cut peeled potatoes into thirds. Place it in the bottom of a big soup pot.
2. After washing the head of cabbage and peeling off the outer layers, cut into 4 parts. Cut those parts into about 2-inch segments. Place the cabbage on top of the potatoes already in the pot.
3. Add water on top of the potatoes and cabbage until they are completely submerged. There should be about an inch of water higher than the potato and cabbage line when you are done.
4. Sprinkle in about 2 teaspoons salt.
5. Bring to a boil on high heat.
6. Once the mixture is boiling, reduce heat to medium and continue to simmer until the potatoes are fork tender. To test this, stick a fork into one of the potatoes. If it slides in easily, then it's fork tender.
7. Have a parent or other adult drain everything into a large colander in the sink.
8. Once the water is drained off, add the cabbage and potatoes back to the pot.
9. Slice the butter into half-inch segments and stir into the cabbage and potatoes.
10. Taste and adjust salt.
11. Serve hot.

MEYER LEMON SHORTBREAD

Makes about 15 cookies

Shortbread is a classic Irish cookie—and guess what? It's super simple to make. Just butter, sugar, and flour. That's it! And the texture? Ohhh my goodness. It's so soft and crumbly it melts in your mouth like magic.

One year, I wanted to mix things up, so I added Meyer lemon juice to the dough. Meyer lemons are like the fancy cousin of regular lemons. They're a little sweeter and a little less sour—kind of like if a lemon and a mandarin orange had a baby. Cool, right?

They grow in Louisiana, which makes them even more special to me! You can sometimes find them at Whole Foods or Trader Joe's when they're in season. But don't worry if you can't—just swap in whatever citrus you have: regular lemons, limes, tangerines, or oranges. It all works!

These cookies are perfect for tea parties, gift boxes... or sneaking one before dinner when no one's looking.

Ingredients:

- 2 sticks unsalted butter, softened
- 1 cup confectioner's (powdered) sugar, divided
- 4 teaspoons zested Meyer lemon peel (Make sure there is no white pith.)
- 3/4 teaspoon Kosher salt, divided
- 2 cups all-purpose flour
- 2 tablespoons Meyer lemon juice

1. In a large bowl or in a stand mixer with the paddle attachment, thoroughly cream the butter, 1/2 cup confectioner's (powdered) sugar and two tablespoons of the zested peel.

2. Combine the flour and salt in a medium bowl.

3. Slowly add the flour mixture to the butter mixture. Stir on low or by hand until completely incorporated. If you're using your hands, you'll need to use your muscles, people!

4. Lay a long sheet of plastic wrap on the counter. Remove dough from the bowl, place it on the plastic wrap, and make it into a log by rolling it in plastic wrap. Refrigerate for at least 40 minutes, or overnight.

5. Preheat oven to 350 degrees. Line a cookie sheet with a Silicone baking sheet or parchment paper.

6. Slice cookies about 1/4 inch thick, and place on cookie sheet.

7. Bake for twelve to fourteen minutes. You do not want these cookies to brown.

8. Remove from the oven and let them cool.

9. Mix the remaining 1/2 cup powdered sugar, Meyer lemon juice, 1/4 teaspoon kosher salt and teaspoon of zest in a small bowl.

10. Once the cookies are completely cooled, brush the tops with the glaze.

*Substitute a good quality vegan butter for a fantastic vegan cookie.

REMY'S ST. PADDY'S DAY SHAKE

Serves 1

You *might've* heard about a certain famous fast-food place that makes a green, minty shake every year for St. Patrick's Day. Well... guess what? Mine is better.

Yep, I said it! Try it and you'll see why. It's cold, creamy, minty, and super fun to make. Plus, you can add your own twist—like whipped cream, sprinkles, or even chocolate chips.

Bonus: No drive-thru line. No waiting. Just shake magic, straight from your kitchen.

So, grab a blender, put on your green, and get ready to make your *own* leprechaun-approved treat!

Ingredients:

- 2 scoops vanilla ice cream
- 1 cup milk
- 1/4 to 1/2 teaspoon mint extract
- Green food coloring
- Whipped cream
- Green sanding sugar or green sprinkles

1. Blitz ice cream and milk in the blender so everything's smooth and creamy. Add the mint extract and a few drops of green food coloring and blend again. Add another couple of drops if the shake's color isn't green enough. Blend again.

2. Pour the shake into the glass.

3. Top with whipped cream and sanding sugar or sprinkles.

4. Serve immediately.

EASTER FUN & FOOD

Spring is *finally* here—time for sunshine, sweets, and fancy dresses.

Easter also means we're heading to my Titi Karen's! Titi Karen is the *coolest*. She's got a candy drawer that never runs out (seriously, it's magical), and her Easter parties are epic. There's a giant egg hunt, a visit from the Easter Bunny, and enough chocolate to last us 'til Halloween (okay, maybe not *that* long).

My cousin Kayden is one of my besties and even helped me test some of the recipes you'll see in this book. So, if you love what you're eating—thank Kayden too!

Secret Family Story Time: One year, my Bubbe decided to *prank* my Uncles Max and Sam. Instead of filling their Easter eggs with candy or money like usual, she stuffed them with... wait for it... mini carrots and broccoli.

They thought they were winning big, and BAM! Veggie surprise! I wish I could've seen their faces. Let's just say, the egg hunt wasn't quite as competitive the next year.

So, whether you're in it for the hunt, the hugs, or the ham, make sure your Easter is full of food, fun, and maybe just a little mischief.

DR PEPPER AND SATSUMA GLAZED HAM

Serves 8

Years ago, *Cook's Country* printed a recipe for a Dr Pepper glazed ham that involved resting the ham at room temperature beforehand, then using a cooking bag and a low baking temperature.

Bubbe took that idea for her Easter ham, wrapping the ham tightly in foil before baking. We keep the Dr Pepper glaze but add Satsuma juice (a delicious citrus from New Orleans).

No matter how you decide to glaze your ham, give this cooking method a try. It results in a tender, juicy ham that everyone will love. Although you can use a spiral sliced ham, we don't. Pre-cut hams tend to dry out when cooking.

Ingredients:

- 1 7-to-10-pound ham
- ¾ cup brown sugar
- 2 teaspoons Dijon or yellow mustard
- ½ cup Dr Pepper
- ½ cup Satsuma juice

1. Remove ham from packaging, including the plastic disc in the center. Place in a baking pan and wrap tightly with aluminum foil.

2. Let it sit at room temperature for 2 hours.

3. Heat the oven to 250 degrees.

4. Place the ham in the oven and cook for 2 hours. Internal temperature should reach 100 degrees.

5. Heat the brown sugar and mustard in a small saucepan on medium heat. Stir to dissolve.

6. Once the sugar has melted and the mustard has incorporated, add the Dr Pepper and Satsuma juice.

7. Continue to cook on low heat for about five to seven minutes or until the sauce has thickened so that it coats the back of a spoon.

8. After the ham has baked for 2 hours, remove from the oven and glaze with half of the sauce.

9. Return to the oven uncovered for an additional 10 minutes.

10. Remove from the oven. Let the ham rest for about 15 to 20 minutes. Slice thin. Drizzle the remaining glaze on top of the slices. Serve.

** Regular cola can be substituted if you don't have Dr Pepper on hand. Orange, tangerine or pineapple juice can be substituted for the Satsuma juice.*

COZY CORN CASSEROLE

Serves 8 to 10

There are *tons* of corn casserole recipes out there, believe me, we've tried a bunch. But this one? This is our family favorite. And once you taste it, you'll totally get why. It's sweet, savory, warm and melty, like a big hug straight from the oven. It's the kind of dish that disappears fast at family dinners, with everyone sneaking seconds (and maybe even thirds). And guess what? It's also crazy easy to make.

Whether you're bringing it to a holiday table or just want something cozy on a rainy day, this corn casserole is pure comfort food magic.

Ingredients:

- 1 stick butter, melted
- 1 cup sour cream
- 2 eggs
- 1 15.25 ounce can whole corn, drained
- 1 14.25 ounce can creamed corn
- 1 box Jiffy Cornbread mix

1. Preheat oven to 350 degrees.
2. Grease a 9×12" pan.
3. Mix all ingredients in a large bowl. Stir just till combined.
4. Pour into the prepared pan.
5. Bake for 40-45 minutes, or until the casserole is set and the edges are brown.
6. Slice into squares and serve.

Lagniappe

Wanna mix it up? Go for it! Some people like to toss in cheese, green chiles, or even swap eggs or sour cream for low-fat stuff. This recipe is super chill—it lets you do you and play around and make it your own!

But just so you know... my Great Aunt Stacey says, "Don't mess with perfection!"

She thinks it's already crazy delicious just the way it is.

REMY'S EASTER EGG CHARBOODIE BOARD

Every time there's a holiday, I tell myself, *"THIS is my favorite!"* But let's be real—Easter might actually win. Why? Because I get to make this *totally awesome, sugar-packed, bunny-approved* Easter Egg Charboodie Board!

Start by popping a few chocolate bunnies on the board (the big kind with the ears, obviously). Then spread out some Easter grass—paper or plastic, whatever makes your board feel like a candy wonderland.

Now… here comes the fun part: Fill in every little space with as many Easter treats as your grown-ups will let you grab from the holiday aisle. Here are my faves:

- Peeps – Some people love 'em, some people don't. I say they're cute, squishy, and belong on every board.
- Jellybeans – The more colors, the better! (But please, *no fart-flavored* ones. We're keeping it classy over here.)
- Malted milk eggs – You know the ones—those speckled candy-coated eggs that melt in your mouth. Instant yum.
- Cadbury eggs – Biting into one and seeing the gooey center is *kinda magical.*
- Flavored chocolate eggs – Strawberry, peanut butter, coconut… yes, please.
- Reese's in egg shapes – Because peanut butter + chocolate = love.
- Decorated Easter cookies – Pretty pastel cookies make your board sparkle.
- Candy corn – But make it *spring colors*!
- Wind-up chicks – Okay, not candy, but they make the board extra cute. Wind one up and let it march across your treats!

Don't forget to snap a pic of your creation and tag me on Insta @chefremypowell. I *have* to see what you come up with!

HOP tO It

Serves 1

Cut the ears off of a hollow chocolate Easter bunny for the best drink container ever!

BONUS: *Eat the chocolate bunny when the drink is done.*

Ingredients:

- 1 hollow chocolate Easter bunny
- Chocolate milk
- Paper straw
- Edible flowers or cotton candy for garnish, if desired

1. Cut ¾ of the ears off of the Easter bunny.
2. Fill bunny with chocolate milk.
3. Add a straw and the edible flower or cotton candy garnish, if desired.

PASSOVER

Passover is an important and special holiday in the Jewish calendar. Families come together for a big meal called a seder, where we read from a book called the Haggadah. Everyone takes turns reading, and the Haggadah tells the story of how the Jewish people escaped slavery in Egypt a long, long time ago.

When the people were leaving Egypt, they had to hurry—and their bread didn't have time to rise. So instead of fluffy bread, they took flat bread with them. That's why, during Passover, we eat matzoh—a kind of unleavened (flat) bread.

One of the *yummiest* things made with matzoh is matzoh ball soup. You crumble up matzoh into a kind of flour called matzoh meal, then mix it into dumplings and drop them into chicken soup.

My Bubbe's chicken soup was the very first real food I ever tasted—and it's still one of my favorites today.

REMY'S LEMON CHICKEN

Makes 8 Servings

This is the recipe that started it all, ya'll. It's the first dish I was ever filmed making and it's what made me want to be a chef. I was only four years old when I started making this dish. I love it so much. It's so easy to make and comes out crispy, juicy and tender. My sisters and I run to get bites of the crackly skin when it comes out of the oven. Yum!

Ingredients:

- 1 whole chicken
- 4 cloves garlic, put through the garlic press
- ½ tablespoon kosher salt
- 1 lemon

1. Preheat the oven to 400 degrees.

2. Remove livers and gizzards from the center cavity of the chickens, reserving for another use, if desired.

3. Place chicken in a roasting pan.

4. Combine the garlic and salt, rubbing together until you form a paste. Gently make a pocket under the skin of the chicken, using your fingers. Be careful not to tear the skin.

5. Carefully stuff the garlic mixture under the skin, then rub what's left on your hands all over the top of the chicken.

6. Wash your hands. If you're like me, you will notice that this mixture has exfoliated your skin, leaving it soft and smooth. Bonus!

7. Pierce the lemon about four or five times with the tines of a fork. Place the lemon in the cavity of the chicken.

8. Put the pan in the oven and roast for an hour or more, until the leg pulls away from the side of the chicken and the juices run clear.

9. Cooking time will depend on the weight of the chickens and the calibration of your oven.

10. Let rest for at least ten minutes before carving. My best advice here is to let an adult carve the chicken. You did the cooking. Let them do the dirty work.

11. Serve with pan juices poured over the chicken.

Lagniappe

1. Fresh herbs such as rosemary and thyme are fantastic on roast chicken. Stuff into the cavity before roasting, if desired.

2. Use the bones, carcass, and any leftover chicken to make leftover chicken soup

3. Bubbe came up with this variation when she had some juice oranges that were about to become too hard to eat. Use an orange in place of the lemon. Amp up the flavor by brushing this maple bourbon glaze on the chicken about 15 minutes before you take it out of the oven.

Maple Bourbon Orange Glaze

- 3/4 cup orange juice
- 1/4 cup maple syrup
- 2 tablespoons bourbon

1. Combine ingredients in a small saucepan. Bring to a boil on medium high heat, then reduce heat to simmer. Simmer until the glaze has thickened. About 5 to 10 minutes.

2. Use to glaze chicken, sweet potatoes, carrots.

LEFTOVER CHICKEN SOUP

Serves 4

This soup can be made from a whole rotisserie chicken if you like. My favorite, though, is to make my lemon chicken for dinner and then have this soup the next day.

Ingredients:

- Bones and carcass from one roasted chicken
- 10 baby carrots, cut into thirds
- 1 medium onion peeled and chopped
- 2 stalks of celery, chopped
- 6 cups chicken stock
- Salt to taste
- A knob of fresh ginger or ½ teaspoon of dried ginger, if desired
- 2 tablespoons fresh dill or 1 teaspoon of dried dill, if desired

1. Place everything in a slow cooker and heat on low overnight or on high until the vegetables are tender and the stock tastes good.

2. Fish out the bones and set the soup aside.

3. Make matzoh balls and boil in water if you would like to add them to the soup. The same thing goes for noodles. Any kind of noodle will work here. I like to use tiny fideo noodles. Always boil your noodles in salted water and then drain. Add to the soup when they are cooked and plump, otherwise they will eat up all of your yummy chicken stock as they expand.

Lagniappe

During Covid quarantine, I hacked chicken soup and came up with Noodle, Noodle, Noodle Soup. We would put it into quart mason jars and deliver it to sick neighbors and friends.

To make Noodle, Noodle, Noodle Soup just add three kinds of noodles to the chicken stock once it's finished. Remember to cook them separately first.

My favorites are cheese tortellini, tiny fideo noodles, and orecchiette—that's Italian for little ears.

Feel free to add leftover chicken to the soup too.

MATZOH BALLS

Makes 10 matzoh balls

Ingredients:

- 4 large eggs
- 6 tablespoons melted butter
- ¼ cup seltzer or club soda
- 1 teaspoon salt or to taste
- ⅛ teaspoon ground pepper
- 1 cup unsalted matzoh meal

1. Beat the eggs in a medium bowl.
2. Add everything except the matzoh meal and mix well.
3. Add the matzoh meal and stir until everything is incorporated.
4. Cover and refrigerate for at least 30 minutes.
5. Meanwhile, bring a large pot filled ¾ the way with water to a boil on high heat.
6. Moisten your hands with water and roll balls into one-inch balls.
7. Drop the balls into the water carefully.
8. Once all of the balls are in the pot, reduce the heat to low.
9. Let simmer for about 30 minutes or until done. When done the matzoh balls will be much bigger and fluffier. If you cut one in half, it should not look dense inside.
10. Remove them with a slotted spoon and place in a bowl until ready to serve. They may be reheated in the microwave before putting into hot soup, if desired.

POT ROAST

Serves 6

This has to be the easiest pot roast recipe ever. It is also one of the best pot roasts you will ever taste. Cooking it slowly at a low temperature makes it so tender that it falls apart. If you can't find Tony Chachere's Creole Seasoning, use a Cajun or Creole seasoning blend that you like.

Ingredients:

- 1 2-pound chuck roast
- 1 ½ teaspoons Tony Chachere's Creole Seasoning
- ¼ cup Worcestershire sauce (We like Lea and Perrins best.)
- 2 ½ tablespoons unsalted butter

1. Preheat the oven to 200°F. (Ask an adult to help with this part if you need!)

2. Grab a small Dutch oven or a heavy pot that can go in the oven. Make sure it has a tight lid and isn't way bigger than your roast—if the pan's too big, the meat might dry out. *No Dutch oven? No problem!* A ceramic baking dish works too—just cover it up tight with foil.

3. Put your roast in the pot or pan and sprinkle Tony Chachere's seasoning all over it.

4. Use your hands (clean ones!) to rub the seasoning into the meat. Get all the sides, like you're giving the roast a spicy little massage.

5. Wash your hands, then sprinkle on the Worcestershire sauce. Slice the butter into thin pieces and place all around the roast.

6. Cover with the lid or tight aluminum foil.

7. Bake at 200 degrees for 8 hours. Test with a fork. The roast should fall apart and there will be a lot of natural gravy to serve alongside it.

Lagniappe

Leftover roast is fantastic for a roast beef po-boy sandwich. Get some French bread, shredded lettuce, sliced tomato and dill pickles. Slather the bread with mayonnaise. (Use vegan mayonnaise if you're kosher.) Heat the roast and gravy and pile on the sliced bread. Top with the lettuce, tomato and pickles and then the other piece of bread. Drink with a Barq's Root beer, to be like a true New Orleanian.

COCONUT MACAROONS

Regular flour is prohibited at Passover. This macaroon recipe is normally made with two tablespoons of all-purpose flour added. I've left that out here, but if you aren't making these for Passover, feel free to add the flour. The cookies will spread less on the baking sheet if you include the flour.

Ingredients:

- One 14-ounce bag sweetened coconut flakes, with 1/4 cup removed
- 1/4 teaspoon salt
- 1 14-ounce can sweetened condensed milk
- 2 teaspoons vanilla extract
- Preheat oven to 350 degrees.

1. Line a baking sheet with parchment paper or a silicone pad.

2. Mix coconut flakes and salt in a large bowl.

3. Add the condensed milk and vanilla. Mix well.

4. Using a small cookie scoop, place the batter onto the baking sheet. Leave at least an inch between the cookies. Some liquids will seep out as they bake.

5. Bake for about 20 minutes or until golden brown.

6. Remove from oven and let cool for just a few minutes. Transfer cookies to a wire rack to finish cooling, removing the excess batter that has spread around the cookies. You may have to re-shape the cookies a little with your hands.

** These cookies are so versatile. They are very sweet, though. To cut the sweetness and make them look prettier, dip half of each cookie into melted semi-sweet chocolate and then place on a parchment or silicone pad lined baking sheet. You can also just drizzle some melted chocolate on top using a spoon or chocolate filled pastry bag. Refrigerate until the chocolate is firm.*

** Make these into thumbprint macaroons by pressing down in the middle of the cookie before baking and filling with your favorite jam. Bake the same as before.*

PURPLE PEOPLE SIPPER

At Passover, adults usually drink sweet purple wine—it's part of the tradition. But my Bubbe makes it fancy by freezing the wine, then adding fruit and fizzy water to make a grown-up slushie. Cool, right?

But guess what? *I started a tradition of my own!* I make a kids' version using purple grape juice—and it's sooo good.

The day before, pour your grape juice into freezer-safe bags or containers and freeze it overnight.

PRO TIP: *Write "Grape Juice" on the bag so no one gets mixed up!*

Ingredients:

- 4 cups purple grape juice
- 1 ½ cup of your favorite chopped fruit – strawberries, grapes, watermelon and peaches work well.
- 2 cups chilled sparkling water
- More fruit for garnishing

1. Combine the grape juice and fruit in a bowl. Pour into a gallon sized zip top freezer bag. Freeze.
2. Take out of the freezer about 30 minutes before you want to serve.
3. Squish the bag with your hands to break up the frozen juice mixture.
4. Divide into 4 glasses.
5. Top each glass with ½ cup of sparkling water. Stir gently.
6. Garnish with more fruit.
7. Serve immediately.

CINCO DE MAYO!

Cinco de Mayo means "Fifth of May" in Spanish. It's a day that celebrates a big win Mexico had way back in 1862—they beat the French army in a battle called The Battle of Puebla. Here's the wild part: people in the U.S. celebrate it even more than people in Mexico!

But let's be real—any holiday with tacos is a YES from me.

It's also a great time to learn about and celebrate Mexican culture. And one of the best ways to do that? FOOD + MUSIC + FRIENDS!

So grab your favorite Mexican snacks, invite your people over, and turn up the Mariachi music (it's my favorite!).

Let's fiesta!

* Frijoles de la Olla
* Guacamole
* Sheet Pan Nachos
* Agua Fresca

FRIJOLES DE LA OLLA

Serves 8 to 10

This recipe is from our friend, Suki Garcia. Suki is an Instagram influencer (@sukisketojourney) and a magnificent cook who specializes in Mexican cuisine and recipes that have been passed down generations from her family in Mexico. She has taught her son, Enrrique to cook as well, taking care to prepare special dishes to keep him healthy. Enrrique has Type 1 diabetes and is on Instagram as @diabeticsuperkid. With his mom's help, Enrrique turned his diagnoses into a superpower.

Your friends will think you have a superpower when you make these refried beans from scratch. They are *ah-mazing* and can be served many ways. Thank you for sharing this with us, Suki!

Ingredients:

- 2 cups mayocoba (Mexican yellow) beans – Find these in the international aisle of your supermarket. If unavailable, substitute pinto or cannellini beans.
- 3 ½ liters water
- 3 garlic cloves
- 1 jalapeno
- Salt to taste

BIG NOTE 1: *Don't add salt at the beginning of this recipe or the beans will be very tough.*

BIG NOTE 2: *If at any point the pot starts to run out of water, boil the new water first and then add to the beans. Adding cold water to the pot will stop the cooking process and darken the beans. This may seem like a lot of water if cooking beans is something you don't do often. Trust me, this is the correct amount of water for this recipe.*

1. Rinse beans in a colander under cool running water. Add beans, garlic and jalapeno to an 8 quart pot. Heat on high. Once the water reaches a boil, lower the heat to medium and cover for 2 hours or until the beans are tender. Salt to taste.

2. This recipe will use all the cooked beans and some of the bean liquid. Once the beans are tender, set a colander over a large bowl, drain the beans but save the cooking liquid.

Refried Beans

- 2 tablespoons avocado oil
- the entire batch of cooked mayocoba bean recipe above
- 1 9-ounce package of chorizo (a type of spicy Mexican sausage)
- 1 cup shredded Monterey Jack cheese

1. Heat a heavy cast iron pan on high heat. Add two tablespoons avocado oil.
2. Break up chorizo (if in links) and fry until it is cooked throughout.
3. Add beans and fry in the chorizo grease for a few moments on medium.
4. Add one cup of water and continue to cook.
5. Once the beans are soft, blend them with a hand blender, potato masher, or immersion blender and blend until smooth.
6. Add 1 to 2 more cups of the bean water, depending on the consistency you like. Turn the heat to medium high.
7. Once the mixture reaches a boil, add one cup of shredded Monterey Jack cheese. Return to a boil and then immediately turn off the heat.
8. Serve as a side dish, dip or filling for burritos, tacos, etc.

Guacamole (aka Guac!)

Serves 4

Okay, let's talk guacamole—because people have *big feelings* about it! Some say guac should always be simple, and others love to toss in tomatoes. Not me. And not Bubbe either. She says tomatoes make it too watery. I just don't like 'em. But here's the deal: you do YOU!

As for me, I add lime juice, cilantro, salt, pepper and garlic powder. Pure perfection.

Ingredients:

- 1 ripe Hass avocado
- Juice of ½ a lime
- 1 tablespoon fresh cilantro, chopped fine
- Salt, pepper and garlic powder to taste

1. Cut the avocado in half and scoop it using a small spoon into a medium bowl.
2. Add the lime juice, cilantro, salt, pepper and garlic powder.
3. Mash using a fork until it is as smooth or as chunky as you like.

SHEET PAN NACHOS

Serves 4 to 6

I make this dish for Bubbe's friends when they come over for girls' night. Originally, I volunteered to cook for girls' night because I thought I could eavesdrop and get some good gossip, but I'll tell you, adult tea is really boring. What's not boring, though, are these spectacular nachos. They are easy to make and everyone loves them.

Ingredients:

HACK: *Use canned refried beans and packaged guacamole for a shortcut*

- 1 large bag restaurant-style tortilla chips
- 2 cups refried beans
- 1 pound shredded chicken, cooked shrimp, cooked and cubed steak or cooked ground meat, if desired
- 1 8-ounce bag Mexican style shredded cheese
- Guacamole
- Salsa
- Shredded lettuce
- Chopped tomatoes
- Pickled or fresh jalapeno slices
- Sour cream

1. Preheat the oven to 350 degrees.
2. Prepare a baking sheet with a sheet of parchment or a silicone pad.
3. Spread the tortilla chips all across the bottom of the baking sheet. It's okay to have them overlap somewhat. There will be leftover chips in the bag. (Don't tell your sisters.)
4. Using a teaspoon, place refried beans on top of the chips all across the baking sheet.
5. Top with whatever meat you decide to use. For a vegetarian version, don't use meat.
6. Sprinkle shredded cheese on top and bake on center rack in preheated oven for 10 minutes or until cheese is melty and the chips are hot.
7. Remove from oven and serve with toppings alongside, so everyone can make their own perfect nacho.

AGUA FRESCA

Serves 1

Agua fresca is a traditional drink that's sold everywhere in Mexico. Not only is it refreshing, but it's a great way to use up fruit that's close to being overripe. Get creative and tag me on Instagram with your favorite fruity combinations.

Ingredients:

- 1 cup fresh fruit, roughly chopped
- 1 cup water
- ½ lime, juiced
- 1 teaspoon sugar

1. Add all ingredients to a blender and blend on high speed until smooth.
2. Pour into a chilled, ice-filled glass.
3. Serve immediately.

** Any kind of melon is great for agua fresca: watermelon, cantaloupe, honeydew, etc.. Strawberries, pineapples and peeled cucumber are excellent too.*

MOTHER'S DAY TEA PARTY

One of my mom Laura's absolute *favorite* things to do is go to a fancy restaurant and have afternoon tea—you know, with tiny sandwiches, cute desserts, and pretty teacups. So, when I wanted to do something really special for her, I thought:

Why not bring the tea party home?

If you have a three-tiered tray, use it to show off all your yummy treats—it makes everything look so fancy! But no worries if you don't—just grab your prettiest plates get creative, and best of all... dress up! Wear a pretty dress, a fun hat, or even a crown.

Because when it comes to afternoon tea, the smaller the treat, the bigger the fun.

And nothing's sweeter than making your mom smile.

- Scones
- Cucumber, Egg Salad and Tuna Salad Finger Sandwiches
- Chocolate-Covered Strawberries
- Tea

SCONES

Serves 8

This recipe has a fun trick: you grate frozen butter right into the flour mixture. It might sound a little weird but trust me—don't skip this step! It's the secret to making your scones super light, fluffy, and totally delicious.

You can switch out the raisins for whatever dried fruit you like best, cranberries, blueberries, or currants all work great. Or skip the fruit altogether if you're more of a plain scone kind of person. Either way, you'll still get a tasty, tender scone with just the right amount of buttery goodness.

Ingredients:

- 2 cups all-purpose flour
- 1/2 cup sugar
- 2 teaspoons baking powder
- 1/4 teaspoon baking soda
- 1/2 teaspoon salt
- 1 extra-large egg
- 1/2 cup heavy whipping cream plus more for brushing
- 8 tablespoons (1 stick) frozen butter
- 1/2 cup raisins

1. Line a baking sheet with parchment paper or a silicone pad.
2. Preheat oven to 400 degrees.
3. Whisk flour, sugar, baking powder, soda and salt together in a large bowl.
4. Mix the egg and whipping cream together in a small bowl.
5. Grate the butter into the flour mixture using a box grater. Be careful not to scrape your fingers.
6. Once the butter is grated into the mixture, use your fingers to mix the dough together until the mixture looks and feels like sand.
7. Pour the egg and cream mixture into the dough and stir gently. Add the raisins.
8. Bring everything together and form a circle about 6 inches in diameter.
9. Place the disc onto the prepared baking sheet. Using a sharp knife, cut the dough into 8 triangular wedges.
10. Separate the wedges so that they are an inch or two apart.
11. Brush the tops with a little heavy cream.
12. Bake in the preheated oven for 18-22 minutes, or until the scones look light, fluffy, and golden brown.
13. Remove from the oven and let cool.
14. Serve with clotted cream (It's a British thing and is super yummy. Order it online.), strawberry jam and/or butter.

CUCUMBER, EGG SALAD AND TUNA SALAD FINGER SANDWICHES

No tea party is complete without finger sandwiches. Finger sandwiches are dainty little treats that you can pick up and enjoy with just two fingers. In my opinion, the ends of the bread must be cut off for the best taste.

You can use white bread, which is traditional. An assortment of breads is nice, too. Consider wheat, rye, pumpernickel—really anything goes. A favorite of mine is slicing mini croissants in half and fill with tuna salad.

For even more fun, you can make your sandwich with whatever square bread you choose and leave the crusts on. Choose a medium-heart or circle cookie cutter and cut out cool sandwich shapes.

The egg salad and tuna salad contain mayonnaise, so it isn't necessary to add mayo to your bread before making the sandwiches. For cucumber sandwiches, however, spread a little butter on the sliced bread before you layer thin slices of peeled cucumber on top.

Aunt Sommer's No-Fail Hard-Boiled Eggs

Okay, real talk: someone in my family made *the worst* hard-boiled eggs for, like... ever. (Spoiler alert: it was Bubbe. Sorry, Bubbe. Love you!) But then Aunt Sommer came to the rescue with her no-fail, super-easy, totally awesome egg method. Now even Bubbe's a pro! Give it a try, you'll get perfect eggs every time. Pinky promise.

1. Bring a pot of water to a rolling boil on high heat. Lower the heat to medium high.
2. Lower eggs gently into the water with a slotted spoon.
3. Set a timer for 12 minutes.
4. After 12 minutes drain the eggs into a colander and immerse them in ice water until they are cool enough to peel.

Egg Salad

Makes about 2 cups

Ingredients:

- 6 hard-boiled eggs, peeled
- 5 tablespoons mayonnaise
- Salt and pepper to taste

1. Place peeled eggs in a medium bowl.

2. Crush with a potato masher or a fork until the eggs are crumbly but not completely smooth. Some people like larger chunks in their egg salad. I like smaller chunks. You decide.

3. Add mayonnaise and salt and pepper to taste. Mix until thoroughly incorporated.

4. Taste and adjust salt and pepper.

** For a little bit of a bite, add 2 chopped scallions to the egg salad at the same time as you add the mayonnaise.*

Tuna Salad

Makes one cup

Ingredients:

- 1 can solid albacore tuna packed in water
- 2 tablespoons mayonnaise
- ¼ cup celery, chopped fine
- Salt and pepper to taste

1. Drain water from the tuna.

2. Mash tuna in a medium bowl with a fork until it is light and flaky.

3. Add mayonnaise, celery and salt and pepper. Mix well.

4. Taste and adjust salt and pepper.

** You may use whatever kind of tuna you prefer, but if it is not solid packed it will yield less. If the tuna is packed in water, you may need to adjust the amount of mayonnaise added to compensate for the extra fat.*

** There are lots of opinions in our household as to how tuna salad should be made. This is the most basic version. My dad adds a little mustard and relish to his tuna salad. I love it. Mom, not so much. This is one of those recipes that you can make your own. Chopped scallions, green or red peppers and water chestnuts are also ingredients you can consider adding.*

CHOCOLATE-COVERED STRAWBERRIES

Why buy expensive chocolate covered strawberries at a specialty grocery store when you can make them yourself? They're easier to make than you would ever guess and taste phenomenal. Make sure you remember to microwave on medium-high, though, or you will end up with burned chocolate.

Ingredients:

- 1 bag of chocolate chips
- 1 quart of strawberries

1. Prepare a baking sheet by layering parchment paper or a silicone mat on it.

2. Wash and gently dry the strawberries with paper towels. They must be really dry. If there are any water drops on the berries, the chocolate won't stick.

3. Get out a microwave safe mug, one that's not too deep so you can dip the berries. Fill the mug with chocolate chips.

4. Microwave on medium power for 2 minutes or until the chips are looking melted.

5. Give them a good stir. The mixture should be creamy and without lumps.

6. Dip the berries one by one about two-thirds of the way into the chocolate. Let the excess chocolate drip back into the mug.

7. Gently place on the prepared baking sheet.

8. Add sprinkles or a zigzag of white chocolate on top if you like. Nuts work too. Make it your own!

9. Chill in the refrigerator until firm.

10. Arrange on a pretty plate or platter to serve. Check out a dollar store near you for some white, heart-shaped or round paper doilies. Line the plate with them before you place the strawberries for a special Mother's Day look.

** The same method can be used to dip pretzel rods or other berries.*

** Use whatever chocolate you like best. Semisweet milk or white. If you are using white chocolate, set the timer for only 1 minute and keep heating in ten second increments until the chocolate is melted. White chocolate burns much easier than milk or semi-sweet.*

TEA (BECAUSE... IT'S A TEA PARTY!)

You can't have a tea party without, well... tea! But guess what? If your mom's not into hot tea (mine isn't either sometimes), no problem! Cheers to being fancy *and* refreshing.

Ingredients:

- 1 tea bag – Get a box of assorted flavors for more fun!
- 8 ounces hot water
- Sugar cubes
- Lemon slices
- Milk

1. Boil 8 ounces of water per tea bag in a tea kettle.
2. Place tea bag in a pretty teacup and pour water on top.
3. Steep for 3 minutes. Do not oversteep or the tea will be bitter.
4. Remove the tea bags.
5. Let each person add their own accompaniments – sugar cubes, lemon slices or milk (like Queen Elizabeth). Serve tea in a pretty tea pot.

** It's a good idea to have at least a few different flavors of tea available. There are many fruity flavors as well as teas without caffeine available, so everyone should be able to find something they like.*

FATHER'S DAY

Not only is my dad the coolest, but he is also an **incredible** cook.

For Father's Day, I thought it would be fun to make one of his special dishes for him.

This menu has some of my all-time favorite foods in it. Gather the ingredients and celebrate your dad with this special menu created just for him.

* Dad's Hamburgers
* Grandma's Blue Ribbon Potato Salad
* Remy's Favorite Cole Slaw
* Root Beer Float Bar

DAD'S HAMBURGERS

This is my dad, Kenton's recipe. Our whole family gets excited when he's making burgers. I love it best when he cooks them on the grill.

Ingredients:

- 1-pound 80/20 ground beef
- Salt
- Pepper

Dad believes the meat should speak for itself. I agree. He adds salt and pepper to taste. Grills to medium-well. Sometimes he puts his thumbprint in the middle to keep the ends from curling up. Good grill marks, tasty beef and a good bun. What could be simpler than that?

Remy's Favorite Coleslaw

Serves 8

Okay, full confession: I'm totally on Team Vinegar Slaw. I love that tangy zip! But if that's not your thing, no worries—you can swap the vinegar for lemon juice for a softer kick, or add 2–3 tablespoons of sugar if you're going for that sweet chicken-joint vibe.

Wanna jazz it up? Ohhh yes you do. Try throwing in fun stuff like sesame or poppy seeds, crunchy noodles or sunflower seeds, tiny chopped orange slices, pineapple bits, sliced scallions, or slivered almonds or a splash of sesame oil for a cool Asian twist.

And here's a party idea: if you're doing a hotdog bar (check out the 4th of July section for more on that), make a few different slaws so everyone can build their own creations. Slaw-tastic!

Ingredients:

PRO HACK: *Use a bag of pre-shredded coleslaw mix and save yourself the mess. Bubbe will thank you.*

- 1 bag coleslaw mix (14–16 ounces)
- 1/4 cup apple cider vinegar
- 1/2 cup mayonnaise
- Salt and pepper to taste

Combine all ingredients in a big bowl and mix well. Refrigerate for at least a half hour before serving.

GRANDMA'S BLUE RIBBON POTATO SALAD

Serves 6

This potato salad was created by my great-great grandma, Laura. Everyone called her G.G. She is the person who first taught my Bubbe how to cook.

Bubbe won a blue ribbon in a 4-H contest when she was my age using this recipe. I make two versions of this for family gatherings because some people I know don't like onions in their potato salad. They don't know what's good for them.

Ingredients:

- 4 medium potatoes (I like Yukon Gold but Aunt Sommer likes russet potatoes. You do you.)
- 4 hard-boiled eggs
- 1/4 cup diced onion
- 1/2 cup diced celery
- 1/4 cup diced olives with pimentos
- 5 tablespoons mayonnaise
- 1 tablespoons apple cider vinegar
- 1 teaspoon salt
- 1/4 teaspoon pepper

1. Cut the potatoes into quarters. Place in a small pot and cover with water. Boil until potatoes are tender. Drain and set aside to cool.
2. Peel then chop hard-boiled eggs into small pieces.
3. Peel the potatoes and chop into small pieces.
4. Combine all ingredients in a large bowl and mix well.
5. Adjust salt and pepper to taste.
6. Garnish with a sprinkle of paprika and sliced olives, if desired.

* *Lemon juice or white vinegar may be substituted for the apple cider vinegar.*

* *If you are a fan of jarred giardiniera, you can substitute it for the olives. The giardiniera pickling juice can also replace the vinegar. Be careful, though. While I love the salad this way, my family found it way too briny.*

ROOT BEER FLOAT BAR

Serves 12

What's better than slurping a root beer float? Making your own float bar, of course! Okay, I say *root beer*, but honestly—you can use ANY soda you love. Seriously. No float shaming here.

Dad's not a root beer guy (I know, right?), but hand him a Mountain Dew float and he's all smiles. Mom's fave? Bright red Barq's cream soda—only found in New Orleans and *soooo good*.

Wanna go wild? Try grape soda, orange soda, or even blue raspberry if you're feeling extra!

Grab some cute cups, scoops of vanilla ice cream, bowls of toppings, and let everyone mix and match. Sprinkles? Whipped cream? Cherry on top? Yes, yes, and yes. It's not just a treat—it's a soda-tastic party in a cup!

Ingredients:

- 12 cans of your favorite root beer or carbonated soda, chilled
- 2 quarts vanilla ice cream, softened to be scoopable
- Maraschino cherries
- Sprinkles
- Whipped cream
- Crumbled cookies
- Straws
- Long spoons
- Fun glasses such as root beer mugs, ice cream sundae bowls, etc.

1. Set everything out on a table, bar cart or tea cart. Make sure you have enough spoons and glassware for everyone. Place the ice cream container in a large ice-filled bowl or punch bowl so it's slow to melt.
2. Add one scoop of vanilla ice cream to the glass.
3. Slowly pour your soda of choice on top, taking care not to let the foam spill over.
4. Top with whatever makes you smile!
5. Add a pretty straw and a long spoon, if you have them.

FOURTH OF JULY – FIREWORKS & FOOD!

Happy Birthday, America! The 4th of July is all about celebrating freedom, fireworks, and fabulous food. It's the *first* big party of the summer after school's out—so bring on the fun!

There are parades, backyard games, red-white-and-blue everything... and don't even get me started on the food. Summer fruits and veggies are *at their best*, which means even simple recipes taste amazing. If you can, hit up a local farmer's market or U-pick farm. It's like treasure hunting for your taste buds.

PRO TIP: *Prep your food early so when the fireworks start, you're not stuck in the kitchen—you're out there with a sparkler in one hand and a strawberry shortcake in the other.*

* Nanie's Corn and Cucumber Salad
* Hot Dog Bar
* Red, White and Blue Crepes
* Fruit Punch with Berry Ice Cubes

NANIE'S CORN AND CUCUMBER SALAD

Serves 6

Ms. Nanie is my best friend on Instagram. She is an amazing chef who specializes in fusion cooking and loves to put her own twist on classic Asian dishes. Ms. Nanie says "Always 'taste test' the food you're cooking. It teaches you how to make connections and become a better cook."

I love this corn and cumber salad from Ms. Nanie because it brought together three of my favorite things: corn, cucumbers and ranch dressing. This salad was the base of the dish that I made when I entered the Florida Future Chef Competition. I added sliced Tajin-marinated chicken and a homemade barbeque sauce to the top of the salad. This dish was chosen as one of the top three and I ended up winning the competition with the recipe I call Sunshine State on a Plate.

Ingredients:

- 1 English cucumber, sliced into thin rounds
- 1 15-ounce can of corn
- ½ small purple onion, sliced thinly
- ½ cup Remy's Ranch Dressing (page 81)
- 2 tablespoons chopped dill
- Salt and red pepper flakes to taste

1. Combine all ingredients in a large bowl and mix until everything is coated with ranch dressing. Taste and adjust for seasonings.

2. Pour into a pretty bowl or platter for serving.

** I love to make this with fresh corn. Remove corn from one cob and sauté in a pan with a tablespoon of butter for about two minutes. Let cool and then it's good to go. Frozen corn works well, too. Just be sure to defrost it first.*

** I prefer sweet yellow onions instead of purple in this salad. But I have to give it to Ms. Nanie. The purple onions look much prettier.*

HOT DOG BAR

We first created a hot dog bar during quarantine. I thought it was one of the coolest ideas ever. It's so much fun to have a large selection of toppings to choose from for your hot dog. All dogs, in my opinion, need a huge pile of crunchy shoestring potatoes on top of them. You can find shoestring potatoes in the potato chip section of your market.

Designing a hot dog bar is fun, too. You can find colorful fast-food type baskets at your local dollar store to serve your dog in. Grab some colorful ketchup and mustard containers while you're there. Consider putting the assorted toppings out in small mason jars. Have fun with it!

I could write an entire book on hot dog toppings. Anything goes, as long as you like it. Here are a few things my family and I like:

- Crunchy shoestring potatoes
- Chili
- Shredded cheese – any kind you like
- Cheese sauce – we like Juanita's brand.
- Coleslaw
- Lettuce
- Tomatoes
- Pickles – sweet, dill, Kosher, sour, half-sour – It's all good!
- Mustard – set out a few kinds like honey mustard, Dijon and Creole
- Ketchup
- Relish
- Guacamole
- Chopped peanuts
- Kimchi
- Thousand Island Dressing
- Cheetos
- Sliced scallions
- Salsa
- Sliced jalapenos
- Sliced radishes
- Chopped cucumber
- And on and on...

RED, WHITE AND BLUE CREPES

Serves 8 to 10

This is an easy recipe for a fancy July 4th dessert. At other times, consider switching out the berries for peaches, blackberries, lemon curd—almost anything goes You could also switch out the Chantilly cream for ice cream. I won't tell anyone if you don't.

Ingredients:

HACK: *1 package prepared crepes*

- 1 tablespoon corn starch
- 2 tablespoons water
- ½ cup granulated sugar
- 1 cup orange juice
- ¼ cup lemon juice
- 1 pint fresh blueberries
- 1 pint fresh raspberries
- 1 pint fresh strawberries, sliced

Chantilly cream

- Confectioner's (powdered) sugar
- Additional berries to garnish

1. To make a citrus sauce, first make a slurry (that's like a thick sauce) with the cornstarch and water by combining them in a small bowl and mixing well. My Uncle Chris calls cornstarch the devil because one time he added cornstarch to a recipe without making a slurry first. He ended up with clumps of white stuff all over the place and ruined the recipe. Don't do that. Cornstarch can be your friend if you treat it right.

2. Add cornstarch slurry to sugar, orange and lemon juice in a small saucepan. Bring to a boil on high heat, then reduce to low until the sauce is thickened – about 10 minutes. Pour into a large bowl.

3. Set aside to cool.

4. Wash and dry the fresh fruit.

5. Make Chantilly cream.

6. Once the citrus sauce is cool, stir in the berries until they are all coated.

7. Lay out the crepes on a clean work surface one at a time. Fill with about 1/4 cup of the fruit mixture.

8. Roll up each crepe, making sure there's fruit throughout the whole thing.

9. Carefully place it on the platter to serve them on.

10. Repeat the process until all of the crepes are filled.

11. Right before serving, sprinkle some confectioner's sugar on top.

12. With a spoon or a piping bag, put a little Chantilly cream on top of each crepe.

13. Garnish with additional berries.

Chantilly Cream

- 1 cup heavy whipping cream
- 2 tablespoons confectioner's (powdered) sugar
- 1/2 teaspoon vanilla paste or 1 teaspoon vanilla extract

1. Beat all ingredients in a stand mixer until the cream is whipped. Take care not to overmix or the cream will get clumpy and start to look like butter.

2. If you have time, chill the bowl of your standing mixer. If you don't have a standing mixer, use a stainless-steel bowl and a hand mixer. This recipe will also work using just a whisk and a bowl, but it will take time and superhuman strength. Just kidding. It takes patience. Lots and lots of patience.

FRUIT PUNCH WITH BERRY ICE CUBES

HACK: *Buy a big gallon of Hawaiian Punch. If you get red punch, make ice cubes with blueberries. If you'd rather get the blue punch, make ice cubes filled with raspberries.*

Ingredients:

- Berry Ice Cubes
- 1 ½ cup water, boiled and then cooled to warm
- 28 raspberries or 42 blueberries

1. Boil the water and let it cool to warm. You don't have to follow this first step, but it will result in a clearer ice cube. Boiling water releases some of the impurities and freezing warm water will form faster.
2. While the water is cooling, fill an ice cube tray with either 3 blueberries or 2 raspberries per section.
3. When the water is warm carefully pour the berries in the tray. Don't fill the squares all the way. Leave about ¼ inch from the top so that the ice cubes have space to expand.
4. Freeze until firm.
5. Pop out of the tray, mix up a pretty drink and say **"Cheers!"**

SLEEPOVER BIRTHDAY PARTY = BEST. NIGHT. EVER.

What's better than a birthday party? One that *literally* never ends—at least until the sun comes up! Welcome to the ultimate Sleepover Birthday Bash, where the fun is nonstop, the food is fabulous, and your BFFs are right by your side.

Now, I've heard stories about how my mom and grandma's sleepovers were all about prank wars, pillow fights, and tossing ice cubes around. Total chaos!

We're way more fabulous than that. My friends and I like to turn the night into a full-on glow-up spa party—think fluffy robes, face masks, nail polish, and lots of giggles. Want to add something extra? Set up a Make-Your-Own Pizza Bar with all your favorite toppings. Way better than takeout (and way more fun)!

And don't forget dessert! The cookie recipe below is the *exact* one I made on TV when I visited Miami's Deco Drive with the awesome host, Alex Miranda. Filming the segment was a total blast.

So grab your coziest PJs, press play on your favorite playlist, and **let the birthday magic begin!**

* Make Your Own Pizza Bar
* Avocado Facials and Cucumber Eye Masks
* Cucumber and Mint Infused Water
* Garbage (aka Kitchen Sink) Cookies

MAKE YOUR OWN PIZZA BAR

HACK: *Buy prepared items and spend your time getting creative with toppings.*

1. Preheat the oven to 400 degrees
2. Choose your base:
    - Prepared pizza dough – find in the refrigerator section of your supermarket
    - Bagels
    - Flatbread
    - English muffins
    - Meatza – ground beef that's smashed as thin as possible and baked in the shape of a pizza
3. Sauce it up:
    - Prepared pizza sauce or your favorite marinara sauce
    - BBQ Sauce
    - Alfredo Sauce
    - Oil and garlic
    - Pesto
    - Ranch Dressing
4. Get cheesy:
    - Mozzarella
    - 6 or 7 blend Italian cheeses – find in the shredded cheese section of your supermarket. This is a family favorite of ours.
    - Ricotta
    - Parmesan
    - Cheddar or a cheddar and Monterey jack blend
5. Veg head:
    - Black or green olive slices
    - Mushrooms
    - Purple or sweet onions
    - Chopped or sliced bell peppers
    - Spinach or arugula
    - The dreaded pineapple
6. Put some meat on it:
    - Pepperoni
    - Tiny meatballs
    - Ham
    - Sausage
    - Turkey or chicken sausage
    - Shredded chicken
    - Ground beef
7. If possible, give each person their own parchment or silicone-lined baking sheet to create their masterpiece.
8. Once the individual pizzas are assembled, bake in the preheated oven on the bottom rack until the cheese is bubbly and the edges of the crust are brown.
9. Serve immediately

***BONUS TIP:** *For extra crispy crusts throw a few ice cubes into the bottom of the oven when you first put the pizzas in to bake. The melting ice will release steam which in turn will make your crust crispier.*

AVOCADO FACIAL

Makes enough for 8 facials

Ingredients:

- 1 avocado
- 2 tablespoons honey
- 1 teaspoon apple cider vinegar

1. Smoosh avocado into a medium bowl.
2. Mix in honey and vinegar until it's a smooth paste.
3. Apply onto your face in a thin layer. Be careful not to get any into your eyes or nose.
4. Take lots of funny pictures while your faces are green.
5. Rinse off when dry.

CUCUMBER EYE MASKS

Makes enough for 8 fancy eye treatments.

Ingredients:

- 1 cucumber washed, chilled and sliced into ¼ inch rounds

1. Put the chilled cucumber slices into a pretty bowl to offer to your guests.
2. Close your eyes and lean your head back a little.
3. Place one slice of cucumber on top of each eye.
4. Chill out to some Taylor Swift music. Discuss the pros and cons of her latest boyfriend.
5. Remove cucumbers after a minute or two and throw them away.

CUCUMBER AND MINT INFUSED WATER

Serves 6

Fancy spas and hotels often serve infused waters. Not only are they beautiful, but they taste much better than just plain water. Cucumber and mint are one of my favorite combinations, but you can use almost any fruits and refreshing herbs you have around. Try strawberries, blueberries, raspberries, lemon or orange slices, watermelon, cantaloupe—or any combination you think would be good.

BIG NOTE: *Prepare these one or two days before serving.*

Ingredients:

- 2 quarts water
- ½ cup mint leaves
- ½ cup cucumber slices

1. Pour water into a pretty pitcher. Add mint and cucumber.
2. Cover and refrigerate at least one day before serving.
3. Serve cold.

GARBAGE (AKA KITCHEN SINK) COOKIES

This is hands down my family's favorite cookie. Sometimes they're hard to find when we make them because certain family members will hide the whole batch. Not kidding. They are that good. The sweet, salty, soft, crunchy combination is a home run.

I had a blast on Miami's *Deco Drive* making these with host Alex Miranda. He is the coolest!

Ingredients:

- 1 17.5-ounce bag Betty Crocker Oatmeal Chocolate Chip Cookie Mix (Plain chocolate chip mix works if you can't find oatmeal.)
- 1 stick butter, melted
- 1 extra-large egg
- 1 cup plain flavored kettle style potato chips, crumbled into smaller pieces (Measure after crumbling.)
- ½ cup peanut butter-flavored chips
- ⅓ cup chocolate chips
- 40 mini pretzel twists

1. Preheat oven to 350 degrees.

2. Prepare a cookie sheet with a parchment paper or a silicone sheet.

3. Pour the cookie mix into a large bowl. Pour the melted butter into the cookie mix and mix slightly. Add the egg and combine thoroughly. You don't want to overmix. When you mix something with a flour base, gluten develops. An overmixed cookie will taste tough.

4. Add potato chips, peanut butter chips and chocolate chips. Mix again.

5. Lay out about 18 of the pretzel twists onto the baking sheet, leaving at least one inch on all sides. You may need two cookie sheets to finish the batch.

6. Using a medium ice cream scoop or a spoon, mound the cookie dough over the pretzels.

7. Top each mound with another pretzel twist and press down.

8. Bake for 12-14 minutes. Cookies may look too soft but they will firm up as they cool. For a softer cookie, bake 12 minutes. For a crunchier cookie, bake 14 minutes.

** Change up the chip flavors here. We use white chocolate or caramel sometimes. Toffee chips are yummy too.*

HALLOWEEN – LET'S GET CREEPY!

Okay, okay... you *probably* know by now that every holiday is my favorite. But Halloween? It might just *win*. Getting ready for a Halloween party is seriously the best. It's the one time in the year when you can be gross, silly, spooky, creepy, and even a little bit weird—and it's all part of the fun!

Hit up your local dollar store for amazing decorations that won't scare your wallet. I'm talking stretchy spider webs, squishy eyeballs, creepy-crawly plastic spiders, and my absolute fave—skeleton hand salad tongs (yes, they exist and yes, you need them).

This is your moment to go wild. Make your food look like brains! Serve punch out of a cauldron! Tape googly eyes on everything!

Don't be *scared*...

Get spooky. Get kooky. Get cookin'.

* Halloween Charboodie Boards and More
* Hot Dog Mummies
* Barfing Pumpkin
* Bloody Hands and Eyeballs Punch

HALLOWEEN CHARBOODIE BOARDS AND MORE

Halloween charboodie boards are the best. There are so many awesome options with this holiday. For a candy board, be sure to include candy corn and other seasonal treats. In the past, we made ghost and bat shaped tiny cookies, chocolate sandwich cookies filled with orange icing and spooky smiley faces, little pumpkin shaped candies and so on. You can cut chocolate graham crackers into gravestone shapes and turn skinny rolled cookies into witch fingers. Just add a little frosting and a sliced almond to the top of the cookie.

A fun idea if you're having a Halloween brunch is to buy some plastic vampire teeth from your local dollar store. Wedge the teeth into the hole in the middle of a bagel. Add some scary eyeballs by sticking candies on with a dab of frosting.

For a savory Halloween Charboodie board, decorate it with some plastic spiders, plastic eyeballs and plastic skeleton hands reaching into the board. Make sure little kids don't have access to this, because we wouldn't want them to choke on plastic.

Hot Dog Mummies

Serves 8 to 10

Ingredients:

HACK: *Use refrigerated crescent dough and packaged hot dogs for an easy entrée that everyone will gobble up.*

- 1 package long hot dogs (We like all beef hot dogs the best.)
- 1 package refrigerated crescent dough
- Candy eyeballs
- Serve with mustard and ketchup, if desired.

1. Preheat oven to 375 degrees.
2. Prepare a baking sheet by lining it with parchment paper or a silicone pad.
3. Open and unroll the crescent dough on a cutting board.
4. Cut long, skinny strips of the dough into about six-inch segments. They should be about ½ an inch wide.
5. Wrap dough around the hot dogs one at a time, leaving space around where you wrap. The dough will expand, and we don't want it to look like a regular pig in a blanket. To get the mummy effect, the strips of dough need to be skinny and there needs to be space.
6. Have fun wrapping. Get as crisscrossed as you want!
7. Place on the prepared baking sheet.
8. When the sheet is full, pop it into the oven on the middle rack.
9. Bake at 375 degrees for 12 to 17 minutes. The dough should be brown and the hot dog hot.

** If you can't find tiny candy eyeballs, dots of mustard will work for the eyes.*

BARFING PUMPKIN

Serves 10

This is my family's favorite version of the classic spinach dip served at parties for years. What makes it special is hollowing out the adorable mini pumpkin. What makes it gross it making it look like the pumpkin is throwing up. Fun!!!

Ingredients:

- 1 mini pumpkin, hollowed out with eyes and mouth carved out
- 1 box frozen, chopped spinach
- 2 cups sour cream
- 1 cup mayonnaise
- 1 envelope dry vegetable soup mix (we love Knorr)
- 1 small onion, finely chopped
- Assorted crackers for serving

1. Defrost spinach and place in a colander. Standing over the sink, squeeze the water from the spinach by the handful. Place the dry spinach in a large bowl.

2. Mix the spinach well and all remaining ingredients except for the pumpkin.

3. Cover bowl and refrigerate for an hour and up to a day.

4. When ready to serve place the pumpkin in the center of a large platter. Fill with spinach dip, ensuring that some of it is pouring out from the pumpkin's mouth. I know. It sounds gross but it looks really cool.

5. Arrange crackers around the platter and serve.

BLOODY HANDS AND EYEBALLS PUNCH

Serves 12

BIG NOTE: *Make the frozen hands at least one day beforehand.*

Serve this scary good punch in a large punch bowl. As with all of my drinks, feel free to make it your own. Add some mango juice or maraschino cherry juice if you have it on hand. Try your new combination in a small glass before you put it in the punch bowl to make sure you like it.

Ingredients:

- 2 disposable latex gloves
- 1 15 ounce can lychee fruit
- ½ pint blueberries
- 1 2-liter bottle lemon lime soda
- 1 64-ounce bottle cranberry cherry juice

1. Fill the latex gloves with water, making sure all of the fingers are full. Leave enough room at the end to tie it off in a knot. Freeze for 24 hours or until completely frozen.

2. Chill all other ingredients until cold.

3. Drain the lychees in a colander. Rinse the blueberries. Insert one blueberry into each lychee fruit, so that it resembles an eye.

4. Fill a large punch bowl with the soda and cherry juice. Gently stir.

5. Take the frozen hands out of the freezer and carefully peel away the gloves. We don't want latex in the punch.

6. Set the hands into the punch and then scatter the lychee "eyeballs" all around.

7. Serve immediately.

HANUKKAH

Hanukkah is a Jewish holiday sometimes called the festival of lights. There was a miracle in which a menorah (candle holder) was lit in the temple and there was only enough oil for it to last for a day. But it lasted eight days. That's why the holiday lasts for eight days, or eight crazy nights, as Adam Sandler says in his popular Hanukkah song.

On Hanukkah, we exchange presents, play a game with a spinning top called a dreidel, and use gelt (chocolates wrapped in gold foil) to bet with. **It's a lot of fun.**

Fried foods are traditional at Hanukkah to remember the miracle of the oil. Latkes, potato pancakes, are one of those treats we look forward to eating all year.

In Israel, fried jelly donuts are a tradition as well. Instead of jelly donuts, I'm giving you a New Orleans hack for an amazing fried donut here. We call them beignets, and I don't know anyone who doesn't love them. We enjoy them doused in confectioner's (powdered) sugar, but you can use honey for a sopapilla taste or granulated sugar mixed with cinnamon for a churro-like bite.

So many choices. They are all good!

* Potato Latke Board/Platter With Smoked Salmon
* Rosemary Applesauce
* Candy Dreidels
* Blue Dreidelade
* Beignets

POTATO LATKE BOARD/PLATTER WITH SMOKED SALMON

Serves 4

If you've ever had breakfast at a Jewish deli, you've probably seen a smoked salmon platter on the menu. It usually comes with bagels, tomatoes, onions, cream cheese—and sometimes even butter (yum!).

But I'm giving it a fun twist! Instead of using bagels, we're stacking everything on top of crispy, golden latkes (those are potato pancakes, and they're *so* good). Think of it like a breakfast tower of deliciousness.

Want to make it even fancier? Add a tiny spoonful of salmon roe caviar on top. It looks super cool and gives a little salty pop in your mouth. (Don't worry—it's fish eggs, but the fun kind!)

Stack it, snack it, and snap a pic before you dig in.

Potato Latkes

BIG NOTE: *Whenever hot oil is being used, keep pets, little brothers and sisters out of the kitchen.*

IT IS IMPORTANT TO ASK AN ADULT TO KEEP WATCH.

Ingredients:

- 2 russet potatoes
- 2 small shallots
- 1 egg
- 1 tablespoon all-purpose flour
- Salt and pepper to taste
- Vegetable oil for frying

1. Peel and grate the potatoes on a box grater. Be careful not to scrape your knuckles.

2. Place the grated potatoes in a clean kitchen towel and squeeze to remove excess water. Grate the shallots.

3. In a medium bowl combine the egg, flour, salt, pepper, potatoes and shallots.

4. Mix using a fork and let sit while you prepare a skillet with oil for frying.

5. Check the temperature of the oil with a thermometer. When it's 350 degrees, you're ready to fry. If you don't have a thermometer, check by dropping a small crouton-size square of sliced white bread into the oil If the bread fries to a golden brown, then the temperature is correct. If it browns or turns black too quickly, the oil is too hot.

6. With a paper towel, blot any excess liquid from on top of the potato mixture.

7. Using a large spoon, place about 1/4 cup of the potato mixture into the oil to fry. Repeat 3 or 4 times around the pan. Be careful not to overcrowd pan. Adding something cold to hot oil will make the temperature go down resulting in a poorly cooked item.

8. When the underside of the latke looks golden brown, turn it over and cook the opposite side until it, too, is golden brown.

9. Remove from frying pan very carefully with tongs, a spatula, or a fork if necessary. Place on a wire rack to cool.

10. Serve immediately.

Buttermilk Herbed Sour Cream

- 1/2 cup sour cream
- 2 tablespoons buttermilk
- 1 tablespoon fresh chives
- 1 tablespoon fresh dill
- 1/4 teaspoon garlic powder
- 1/4 teaspoon onion powder
- Salt to taste
- Pepper to taste

Mix all ingredients together in a small bowl. Refrigerate for at least 30 minutes before using.

Pickled Red Onions

- 1/2 small red onion peeled and thinly sliced
- 1/2 cup apple cider vinegar
- 1/8 cup water
- 1/2 teaspoon salt
- 1 tablespoon sugar

Place all ingredients in a small saucepan on high heat. Bring to a boil and then turn off. Let the onions steep in the hot liquid for at least 30 minutes. Drain off the liquid, place in a covered container and refrigerate until ready to use.

There are so many fun things you can serve with potato pancakes. Here are just a few suggestions of things you can use to make a pretty platter: Salmon roe caviar, Smoked salmon, Small capers, Lemon, Watermelon radish, Fresh dill, Fresh chives, Cucumber.

Lagniappe

One of my favorite restaurants, 3 G's in Delray Beach, Florida, serves a brisket sandwich with a potato pancake on top of the meat. You could do this using some leftover pot roast from my Passover recipe. Get some brioche or challah buns if you can. Don't forget to spoon on some gravy. You can thank me later.

ROSEMARY APPLESAUCE

Serves 4

You *could* grab a jar of applesauce from the store—and it'll be fine. But if you want to make your latkes go from "yum" to whoa, try this version made with fresh apples, a drizzle of honey, and a sprig of rosemary. It's a little sweet, a little herby, and totally worth the tiny bit of extra effort. Trust me on this one.

Wanna hear a funny story? One Hanukkah, my mom and her cousins were at their grandma's (they called her Safta—that's the Hebrew word for grandma) and Safta had made a big plate of crispy potato pancakes. But—uh oh—no applesauce! That's a Hanukkah no-no. So what did they do? They ran around her apartment building knocking on doors asking neighbors if they had any applesauce to spare. Can you believe it? Finally, a kind neighbor came through with a jar. Total applesauce miracle!

P.S. *Please don't go knocking on random doors asking for applesauce today. That's not exactly a safe or smart idea. Let's stick to the recipe instead.*

Ingredients:

- 3 whole apples, peeled, cored and chopped
- ¼ cup water
- 2 tablespoons honey
- 2 teaspoons fresh rosemary, finely chopped
- ⅛ teaspoon salt

1. Combine all ingredients in a medium saucepan and give everything a good stir. Heat on high until the mixture comes to a boil. Immediately lower to simmer and cook for 15 to 20 minutes longer. The apples should be falling apart but not completely mushy.

2. Add a few spoons of water at a time if the mixture isn't fully cooked but looks dry.

3. Taste and adjust the honey. Depending on the type of apple you use and your personal taste, more honey may be necessary.

4. Remove from heat and cool.

5. Store in a covered container in the refrigerator until ready to use.

Candy Dreidels

Ingredients:

- Jumbo marshmallows
- Pretzel sticks
- Nutella or frosting
- Hershey Kisses, unwrapped
- Melted chocolate for dipping, gel frosting for piping or sprinkles if desired

1. Carefully slide a pretzel stick into the round end of a jumbo marshmallow, taking care that the pretzel doesn't come out of the other side of the marshmallow.

2. Using a little Nutella or your favorite frosting "glue" the unwrapped Hershey's Kiss to the end of the marshmallow opposite the stick.

3. Let dry for about 10 to 15 minutes.

4. Dip the "dreidel" into melted chocolate or check the internet for examples of Hebrew letters that you can pipe on the side of the dreidels with piping gel. Bling it out with sprinkles if you like.

5. Arrange on a pretty platter and serve.

Blue Dreidelade

Serves 1

Blue and white are the colors of Israel, and the colors most people use to decorate for Hanukkah.

My favorite way to make blue drinks is to get some non-alcoholic blue Curacao syrup from the beverage aisle at the supermarket. You can buy it online too.

Blue Curacao has an orange flavor, and it's one of the first ingredients I ever used to make drinks with. I used to sneak it out of Bubbe's fridge and turn all of my drinks blue when I was 4 or 5.

You can find blue maraschino cherries online as well. Blueberries are great for blue drinks too. Frozen blueberries are even better, because they will keep your drink cold longer.

Because blue Curacao is sweet, I like to add it to flavored sparkling water. Fill a chilled glass with ice, add your favorite flavor of sparkling water and then drizzle the blue Curacao into the glass and stir gently. Garnish with some chocolate "gelt" and say "*L'chaim!*" That's a Hebrew cheer and it means "To life!"

Beignets

Serves 6

HACK: *Make beignets (New Orleans style donuts drenched in confectioner's sugar) out of canned biscuit dough.*

Ingredients:

- 1 can large flaky biscuit dough such as Pillsbury Grands
- Canola or vegetable oil
- Confectioner's (powdered) sugar

1. Place two inches of oil in a heavy saucepan and heat on medium to 350 degrees.
2. Cut each biscuit into 4 triangles.
3. Place into the oil with care and fry for two to three minutes, flipping them over and frying the opposite side when they look golden brown.
4. Remove with a slotted spoon and drain on a paper towel lined plate.
5. Sprinkle tons of confectioner's (powdered) sugar on top.

HACK: *If you don't have a thermometer to check the temperature, put a little square of white bread into the oil. If it burns quickly the oil is too hot. If it sinks into the oil and bubbles aren't forming around it, the oil is too cold. If it begins to turn golden after a minute or two, then the oil is the perfect temperature.*

HACK: *Throw a few of the beignets into a small paper bag and sprinkle some sugar into the bag. Close the top and shake it like a Polaroid picture.*

** Don't wear black while making beignets. Seriously. Half the fun of eating them is getting sugar everywhere!*

CHRISTMAS MORNING

There are so many amazing things about Christmas. No school. Gifts from Santa. Fun times with our families.

To me, preparing for Christmas is a big part of the fun. During the week before the holiday we make cookies and a gingerbread village made of Pop Tarts. Watch out for elves, little sisters and cousins, though. If you're not paying attention parts of your village will start to disappear every night when you're asleep.

When I was little, I would leave out cookies and milk for Santa on Christmas Eve. Over time I realized that Santa might like a healthy snack, considering all of the houses he's visiting and all the cookies he's enjoying. A few years ago, I began to make him my special ranch dressing served with baby carrots and celery sticks. By adding vegetables, even the reindeer can have a treat.

Now, onto one of the most important traditions: **Christmas breakfast.**

This is a great time to get creative and really enjoy yourself.

LOST BREAD

Serves 6

What was once lost but now it's found? Lost bread! That's what we call *pain perdue*, or French toast, in Louisiana. Our family loves this special treat, and it's a great way to use up stale bread. It doesn't let anything go to waste and saves money too!

Ingredients:

- ¾ cup whole milk
- 2 eggs
- 1 teaspoon vanilla extract
- 1 teaspoon ground cinnamon
- Pinch salt
- 6 slices white bread (a few days old), French, Challah, or Italian bread. Any dense bread works, but it must be stale.
- 2 tablespoons unsalted butter

Optional toppings:

- Sliced strawberries
- Blueberries
- Maple syrup
- Confectioner's (powdered) sugar

1. Whisk together the ingredients in a shallow bowl and set aside.

2. Lightly grease a griddle or skillet with butter over medium-high heat. While it heats, dunk the bread in the egg mixture and soak both sides.

3. Fry the slices of the bread on the skillet over medium heat until golden-brown, about 3 minutes per side.

4. Serve hot with maple syrup, butter, or any toppings your family loves. It's also fun to offer a choice of toppings.

HOT CHOCOLATE BAR

Serves 4

HACK: *Use premade hot chocolate mixes or hot chocolate pods made for the coffee machine.*

Homemade Hot Chocolate

- 4 cups whole milk or nut milk of choice
- 1/4 cup granulated sugar
- 1/4 cup cocoa powder
- 4 ounces semisweet chocolate chips
- 2 teaspoons vanilla extract

1. Combine all ingredients in a medium saucepan and heat to a boil on medium heat. Reduce to low and simmer, stirring, until everything is smooth and incorporated.

2. Fill mugs 3/4 the way full with the hot chocolate, leaving room for add-ins.

Add-ins:

- Marshmallows in different sizes
- Flavored marshmallows
- Peppermint sticks
- Cacao nibs
- Whipped cream
- Chocolate syrup
- Sprinkles or sanding sugar
- Cookie mug toppers
- White chocolate or dark chocolate shavings
- Pirouette (long, skinny) cookies – Find in the cookie aisle of your supermarket.
- Caramel syrup
- Rock candy stirrers
- Crushed peppermint
- Coarse sea salt

POP TART VILLAGE

Raise your hand if you've ever tried to put together a boxed gingerbread house and it fell apart. I'm raising my hand really high over here. I'm not sure why it's so hard to get those walls to stick together, but I have a solution for you. Use Pop-Tarts! The strawberry frosted ones seem to work best for Christmas, so I would recommend those.

Ask an adult to help you cut the Pop-Tarts to make a roof, if necessary. My Uncle Chris does an amazing job of that for our family.

Finish building your Pop-Tart house using royal icing as "cement," then decorate the house with whatever candies you like—peppermints, M&M's, gumdrops, Nerds. Holiday colored sprinkles are fun too. If you like it, use it!

We have had fun building our own individual Pop-Tart houses and then putting them all on a big board or large baking tray. To make a village add things like seasonal tree-shaped and gingerbread cakes. Little Debbie makes some cool ones. You can also use things like peppermint sticks, marshmallows and hard candies to make things like walkways.

HACK: *Use a glue gun to make it easier to get your Pop-Tart house to stay together. Make sure everyone knows not to eat it. This will just be for decoration.*

Easy Royal Icing

- ½ cup confectioner's (powdered) sugar
- 2 to 3 tablespoons water

In a small bowl, mix sugar and water together until it's smooth and the consistency of glue. Use immediately.

NEW YEAR'S EVE PARTY

There are so many things I love about New Year's Eve!

One: You get to stay up *way* past bedtime.

Two: There's always something sparkly.

Three (okay, the best one): **The snacks!**

Some families do big fancy dinners for New Year's Eve, but at our house, it's all about finger foods. We fill the table with fun little bites and keep extra snacks in the fridge so we can add more as the night goes on. Veggie trays, mini sandwiches, charcuterie boards—yum! Some are super healthy, and some are just plain *treat-yourself* snacks. And the best part? They make awesome leftovers you can snack on all week.

Total win.

* CRUDITÉ PLATTER WITH REMY'S RANCH DIP
* CHARBOODIE BOARD
* Cheese Ball
* Sparkling Station

CRUDITÉ PLATTER WITH REMY'S RANCH DIP

Serves 8

Say it with me: "crew-deh-TAY!" It's a fancy French word that really just means raw veggies. I found out that back in the 1960s and 70s, crudité platters with dip were super popular at parties. Here's a secret—I actually like raw veggies *way* more than most cooked ones. Especially when there's ranch dip. Ranch makes everything better.

The first dip I learned to make was ranch. It's kind of like ranch dressing, just thicker—and perfect for dipping veggies, chips, or even pizza crust (yep, I said it). Here's something wild: the very first ranch dressing was invented in Alaska by a plumber who became a cowboy. Whaaaat?! How cool is that?

When I made my first batch, I just used what we had at home. We had fresh dill but no parsley or chives, and we didn't have buttermilk either. So I made a shortcut version with milk and a little vinegar—boom! Still super tasty.

But if you're making this for a party or something special, try it with *fresh* dill, parsley, and chives—and real buttermilk. It takes the dip from yum to *ah-mazing*.

Remy's Ranch Dip

- ½ cup buttermilk
- ½ cup sour cream
- ½ cup mayonnaise
- 1 tablespoon chopped dill
- ½ teaspoon onion powder
- ¼ teaspoon garlic powder
- 1 tablespoon dried parsley (or 2 tablespoons fresh)
- 1 tablespoon dried chives (or 2 tablespoons fresh)
- salt and pepper to taste
- juice of ½ lemon

1. Combine ingredients in a large bowl.

2. Whisk it all together ("Whisk" is a fancy word and a tool for mixing ingredients together really well). Add a little salt and pepper—taste it and see if you want more. Then cover it up and pop it in the fridge. It gets even yummier after it chills for about an hour, so try to be patient (I know, it's hard!).

Lagniappe

To make homemade buttermilk, add one tablespoon of vinegar or lemon juice to one cup of whole milk. I like vinegar better than lemon juice here, but both will work. Mix them together and leave alone for about 10 minutes. You will see the milk looks curdled. That's when it's ready to use.

If you add some peeled and medium diced cucumber to this ranch, it makes a fantastic tzatziki (Greek dip).

Now for the fun part—picking your veggies!

You get to choose your favorite raw veggies for the crudité platter. I'm *not* a fan of tomatoes (ew), but most people love them—so I still add them. The little grape or cherry ones work best. If you can find the heirloom kind with all the fun colors, your platter will look extra cool.

Now cucumbers? That's a different story. My sisters and I always fight over the last slice—so I pile on *lots*. If you can find English cucumbers, use those! They're seedless and nice and crunchy. Total cucumber win! Baby carrots are a must. If you can find the rainbow ones, that looks really cool.

Lots of people like broccoli and cauliflower cut into bite-sized pieces. This can make a big mess, so be careful. Make sure you have an adult help with the cutting and use a large cutting board.

Celery sticks are also important. I don't know anyone who doesn't love celery with dip. My Uncle Chris will eat an entire bag of celery sticks all by himself. Make sure you cut enough.

Other fun items to put on the platter are radishes, snow peas and sugar snap peas.

Assemble the Platter

Line the bottom of the platter with soft, pretty lettuce such as butter lettuce if you have it.

Then arrange the vegetables in little groups on top of the lettuce, placing the dip in a cute bowl in the middle or to one side of the platter.

This is where you can get creative. Think about what colors look good next to each other and what shapes the vegetables will be in. Even little sisters or brothers can help with this part.

If you want to get extra fancy, hollow out bell peppers or even a whole cauliflower to make a bowl for the ranch dip.

Cut off the bottoms of the peppers or cauliflower so it sits flat, then hollow out the middle of the vegetables and fill with dip.

Then arrange the other vegetables around that.

CHARBOODIE BOARD

I've shown you how to make fun, sweet Charboodie boards for Valentine's day, Easter, and Halloween. Now it's time for the one that inspired all of those—the classic savory (that means salty and cheesy instead of sweet) charcuterie Charboodie.

Making a Savory Charboodie Board

If you're going for a savory vibe, here's what I like to do:

1. Start with at least two types of meat—salami and pepperoni are my go-tos. I love folding the salami into little rose shapes. It's super easy! Check out my video on Instagram @chefremypowell to see how I do it.

2. Next, add a few kinds of cheese (soft, hard, or both!), some fruit like grapes or apple slices, one or two kinds of nuts, and a bunch of crackers. Mix it up and make it fun. Easy, peasy and good!

3. For a candy board, bring your besties and brothers and sisters to the store to choose the goodies. Trust me, we know what the best choices are. Arrange things by color, shape and size. Use cute little bowls to hold small items or dips.

Want to make your board extra fun for the holidays?

Go all out with holiday-themed goodies! Pick candy, fruit and snacks that match with the colors, shapes and flavors of the holiday: like fresh raspberries and blueberries for the 4th of July or candy canes and Santa-shaped chocolates at Christmas. You can even match your dips and snacks to the holiday—like pink frosting with cookies or pastel-colored crackers.

With boards like this, people won't just come to your party—they'll *run* to your party. Everyone loves my snack boards, so our house is always packed. (Seriously, you should see it!)

REMY'S CHEESE BALL = PARTY VIBES

Serves 8

My Bubbe says cheese balls were a *huge* party food in the 1980s. She'd say that back then, everyone was listening to Madonna, rocking side ponytails, and growing chia pets. (Yep, that was a real thing.) You don't *have* to wear a side ponytail or blast '80s music while you make this... but honestly? It makes it way more fun.

Most cheese balls start with cream cheese. Then you mix in other cheeses and fun flavors—whatever you're into. Sweet, savory, spicy—it's your cheese ball, so go wild!

Ingredients:

- 8 ounces cream cheese
- 8 ounces shredded Colby jack and cheddar blend
- ½ teaspoon onion powder
- ½ teaspoon garlic powder
- 1 tablespoon chili oil
- 2 scallions, diced
- ¾ cup sliced almonds

1. Add everything except the nuts to the food processor. Pulse until well-combined.
2. Lay a long sheet of plastic wrap on the counter and spread out the nuts.
3. Dump the cheeses mixture onto the nuts and roll into a ball, using the plastic wrap to help you.
4. Refrigerate for about two hours, or until firm. Unwrap and put on a pretty platter.
5. Serve with crackers, French bread or even bagels!

Remy's Notes:

The first time I made this, I just used whatever I found in the fridge—and guess what? It still turned out awesome. You can totally do the same! No fancy cheese blend? Just use plain cheddar or Colby Jack. Don't like spicy? Skip the chili oil. Want a little kick but don't have chili oil? Try a tiny bit of cayenne pepper (like ¼ teaspoon) or a splash of hot sauce instead.

No scallions? Use chopped onions or shallots. And feel free to switch up the nuts, too—pecans taste *so* good on a cheese ball. Once you've got the basics down, you can mix and match and make it totally your own. That's the fun part!

SPARKLING STATION

Brunches, baby showers, and fancy parties always seem to have something called a mimosa bar. (At least that's what the ladies in my family say!) It's basically Champagne or sparkling wine with different juices and fruit you can mix in. It looks super pretty—but I've never tasted one, obviously.

But here's the thing: why should adults have all the fun?! On New Year's, they get to do a big toast with bubbly, so I say... let's make our *own* sparkling station! Grab some sparkling grape juice or fizzy lemonade and mix it with fun juices and fresh fruit. It's sparkly, it's sweet, and it's all ours. Let's do this!

Remy's Sparkling Station Instructions

Ready to throw the ultimate fizzy party? Let's set up a Sparkling Station that'll make everyone feel fancy—even without Champagne!

Step 1: Pick your party spot.

Clear off a table, tea cart, or bar cart. This is your sparkle zone!

Step 2: Make a fun sign.

Use a chalkboard or poster board and write the Sparkling Station Rules:

A. Pour your bubbles

B. Add your favorite juice

C. Top with fruit or edible flowers

Decorate the sign with stickers, glitter, or doodles—it's part of the fun!

Step 3: Grab the cutest glasses you've got.

This is your time to shine. Fancy cups = fancy vibes. (Plastic ones work too—just add a cute straw!)

Step 4: Pour the juice party!

Put different juices into cool pitchers or carafes. I love cranberry, peach, and orange, but you do you!

Step 5: Fruit explosion time.

Fill small bowls with colorful fruit—blueberries, raspberries, strawberries, orange slices, whatever you love. If you find edible flowers, *bonus points*! They make everything look like a fairy tea party.

Step 6: Keep it chill.

Put your sparkling grape juice in a bucket of ice so it stays nice and cold.

Step 7: Don't forget the most important part...

Raise your glass and say, ***"Cheers!"***

ACKNOWLEDGEMENTS

The biggest thanks to my grandmas, who really made this book come together. Thank you, Coco and Bubbe.

Thanks to my mom and dad, Laura and Kenton Powell for always supporting me in everything. Thanks also to my sisters, Rory and Lil Laura Powell. They are the best sous-chefs and friends.

Many thanks to Kit Wohl for her mentorship and the incredible amount of work she did to make my book dream a reality.

I have many relatives who have supported me in so many ways. From sending me cool kitchen tools to taking me out for wonderful meals to letting me experiment in their kitchens, to traveling all the way to California for the Master Chef Junior finale—they are always there for me. Thanks to Stacey Broussard, Sommer Duhon, Sue and Dave Fischer, Wanda Galarza, Robert Goldman, Patricia and Ted Johnson, Rosemarie Powell, Julie Raines, Jessica Reab, Joey Schultz, Lisa Silverberg, Max Silverberg, Sam Silverberg and Zan Strumfeld.

The Krewe of 32 are my friends, my neighbors and my biggest cheerleaders. Thanks to Chris, Caroline, and Olivia Bernal, Becky, Laura, and Adelaide Wyness, Kathryn Rodgers, Diana Halden, Eamonn and Kate Fitzgerald.

Thanks to all of my recipe testers as well. I appreciate you all! Leia Dwyer, Richard Dwyer, Karen Ferro, Kayden Jones, Brendon, Emma and Sophie Powell, Amaya Seegobin and Michael Seegobin.

My experience on Master Chef Junior was a dream come true. There are so many people to thank here that this book would be 500 pages if I could name and thank them all. Forgive me if I missed anyone.

Many thanks to the Master Chef Junior judges, Gordon Ramsay, Tillie Ramsay, Aaron Sanchez and Daphne Oz. The time we spent together and your mentorship are priceless gifts. Gordon is a loving, kind, incredible human being who not only made me grow as a chef but made me laugh every time we were filming together. I love him like a dad.

Tilly is cool, sweet, fun and a fashion icon! She is also an amazing chef and mentor.

Aaron and I share Latin heritages and a love for everything New Orleans. His culinary advice and mentoring raised the bar for me.

Daphne Oz was our substitute mom on set. She is not only smart, sweet and beautiful but she made sure to mention every good thing I did in the kitchen. How fabulous is that?

Thank you to producers Patrick Reina and Danny Schrades for making my journey possible.

Special thanks to producer, Nicole Rosen, who was there for me in so many ways. Thanks also to producers Lauren McKay and Stephanie Waters. I really appreciate how hard you all worked to make sure we not only had fun, but were at the top of our game.

To Jaycee Medina, Vice-President extraordinaire at Endemol Shine. Thank you for your expert help and guidance.

Thanks to Louise Leonard and the entire culinary team at Master Chef Junior.

Thanks to Danielle Dreben, Carl B. Thompson, and to all the wranglers.

Thank you to the kids I competed with on Master Chef Junior. Alfred Eggermont, Kristell Jean, Jordyn Joyner, Lydia Ledon, Bryson McGlynn, Asher Niles, Miles Platt, Michael Seegobin, Jason Sun, Lilo Tsai and Breanna "Bre" Williams.

Thank you to Ace Adler, Ariel Strickland, Serena Seggern and Candace Smith.

Special thanks to Chef Sabrina Courtemanche for her mentorship and friendship.

Thank you to Phil and Kate Marro, founders of the Visit Lauderdale Food and Wine Festival.

Thank you to John Dufresne for your help in proofreading this book.

To the team at the Florida Future Chef Competition sponsored by the Florida Department of Agriculture and Consumer Services. Special thanks to Vianka Colin, Jeremy Eason, Selby Proctor and Chef Jorje Sanchez.

Special thanks to Leon C. Brunson, Suki Garcia, Ellen Kanner and Nanie Ware for inspiring me and providing recipes and guidance.

Finally, thank you to my future husband, Walker Scobell.